A RUNNERS GUIDE TO O'AHU

A RUNNERS GUIDE TO O'AHU

Richard W. Varley

MAPS BY
Shingo Matsushima

A LATITUDE 20 BOOK
UNIVERSITY OF HAWAI'I PRESS ◆ HONOLULU

© 2004 University of Hawaiʻi Press

All rights reserved

Printed in the United States of America

09 08 07 06 05 04   6 5 4 3 2 1

LIBRARY OF CONGRESS CATALOGING-IN-PUBLICATION DATA
Varley, Richard W.
  A runners guide to Oʻahu / Richard W. Varley ; maps by
  Shingo Matsushima.
    p. cm.
  "A Latitude 20 book."
  ISBN 0-8248-2793-7 (alk. paper)
  1. Running—Hawaiʻi—Oʻahu—Guidebooks. 2. Oʻahu (Hawaiʻi)—
  Guidebooks. I. Title.
  GV1061.22.H39V37 2004
  796.52′09969′3—dc21
                                        2003055274

University of Hawaiʻi Press books are printed on acid-free paper
and meet the guidelines for permanence and durability of the
Council on Library Resources.

To my parents, H. Leslie and Margaret Varley,
for their tremendous love and support,
and to Coach Ray Herman,
who instilled in me a love of running

CONTENTS

PREFACE

In 1987, an old college buddy of mine, Scott Nakahara, challenged me to run the Honolulu Marathon with him. I had been a sprinter in my high school and college years, and I always enjoyed running, but to me any race longer than 0.25 mile was simply out of the question.

After weeks of assailing my ego, I finally gave in to Scott's prodding and started a serious training regimen for conquering my first marathon. Of course, "serious" is a relative term. At the time, I thought extending my 3-day-a-week runs from 3 miles to 5 miles was pretty darn serious, and I had no idea what I was getting myself into.

The evening before the marathon, I went out with Scott and his fiancée, Susan, for my very first carbo-loading—I never had to do much carbo-loading for a 400-meter race—and we sat down to plan our strategy. Our goal was to break 5 hours, so we decided to begin at a slow, comfortable, 10-minute-per-mile pace and just hold on for as long as possible. We felt it was important to stick together and motivate each other when the miles started to add up.

Despite our planning the night before, our strategy took a big hit within the very first mile of the marathon, when Scott twisted an ankle on a wet street reflector. He hung tough through the pain for the next 12 miles. At that point, the pain had spread to his knee, and he was forced to walk. I continued on, completely unsure of how to pace myself for the remaining 14 miles.

I could describe all my suffering or how I felt when a guy passed me wearing Japanese *getas* (wooden slippers set up on 3-inch blocks), but I'll save you from the gory details. I completed the full 26.2 miles, and I succeeded in breaking the 5-hour barrier by a full 28 seconds. Scott finished about an hour behind, overcoming what was later diagnosed as a stress fracture in his ankle. However, despite our pain, completing a marathon made me hungry for more. The adrenaline rush was addictive, and I was determined to develop a more structured training program that would allow me never to settle for a 5-hour marathon again. I was hooked.

Unfortunately, reality set in, and, truth be told, I was still a sprinter at heart, which meant I was basically lazy, and I always had a litany of excuses for skipping my long training runs. So there I was, with a passion to compete in marathons but without a passion for training. Finally, I devised a solution and started my own running club at the University of Hawaiʻi. This club was designed to bring my fellow faculty together with students, providing a great support system and helping us all get into competitive condition.

As the president of the Mānoa Road Runners, I felt obligated to show up for every training session, and I finally saw my mileage climb to 30, then 40-plus miles a week. That mileage still wasn't great, but it was certainly much more realistic in order to run marathons. Another benefit I gained from running with this group was that I was introduced to a variety of new running courses on a weekly basis. The group got tired of running the same routes over and over again, so we began the search for new ones. This search led to the realization that there was a definite need for a comprehensive guide to running routes on Oʻahu.

ACKNOWLEDGMENTS

Many people have been instrumental in helping me put this book together. First is my editor at the University of Hawai'i Press, Masako Ikeda. Masako is a runner, and we had trained together a few years ago. She asked if I would be interested in writing a guidebook for running on O'ahu, and I immediately jumped at the opportunity. I had discussed this idea with some of my running partners, and I was thrilled when she called me. My copy editor, Caroline Roberts, also did a tremendous job to make it look like I had paid attention during my English classes.

My training partners in the Mānoa Road Runners—Doug Smith, Dennis McDougal, Jerry Finin, Bill Turner, Tomas and Cindy Cummings, Warren Takenaka, Robert Harris, Ian Kubo, and Cam Shuford, just to name a few—have provided me with much support and advice. They have made it fun to search out all the great running locations described in this book. I am fortunate to be surrounded by such intelligent, funny, and competitive folks.

Scott Roy, a schoolteacher and triathlete extraordinaire, took time to take me around Mililani and Mililani Mauka to show me his favorite neighborhood training routes. Steve Foster of Timers Plus, another triathlete friend, also helped by showing me all his favorite routes around 'Ewa Beach.

Ray Woo at Runner' HI has always been available with excellent advice and encouragement and is a real professional and friend. I would also like to thank Raul Boca, O'ahu's foremost triathlete, triathlon coach, and race director. Raul does everything with the utmost skill and class. Without Raul, I doubt I would have ever tried a triathlon, but after competing in just one of his events, I knew I was hooked. Chet "the Jet" Blanton, a good friend, also helps me keep all my training and competitive spirit alive and in perspective. Thanks also to Debbie Hornsby, a former national amateur champion triathlete, for her help in describing her favorite training spot, the Tantalus Trails. These trails are indeed her passion.

Beyond the text, the true value of this book is in its clear and precise maps. Shingo Matsushima of Rōnin LLC worked tirelessly on their creation and design. He worked late into the night and put aside much of his own work to complete these maps within my tight time frame.

Last, but definitely not least, I wish to thank my wife, Mitsue, who has provided the encouragement—and sometimes the kick in the pants—to keep me on track, and she has always been there with positive reinforcement for my writing, as well as my training and my races. My two most memorable marathons were the two I ran with Mitsue. Her strength and determination never fail to amaze and motivate me.

INTRODUCTION

RUNNING ON O'AHU O'ahu is a terrific place to run and train. The island is blessed with a moderate tropical climate that varies little throughout the year. The months of December through February are the island's rainy season, and the average high temperature is 78 degrees (25°C). August and September tend to be the hottest months, when the cooling trade winds slow, and the heat and humidity builds. During this period, the average high temperature is 87 degrees (29°C) with the potential for 90-plus percent humidity. During the hottest months, try to schedule your runs in the early morning or after sundown. Other options would be to schedule more trail runs or select higher elevations to avoid the excessive heat. Visitors to the islands will notice an increase in humidity year-round, but the prevailing trade winds usually provide refreshing offshore breezes to make it manageable.

The windward side of O'ahu faces the prevailing trade winds and, as a result, is normally breezier and cooler than the leeward side of the island. The windward side is also much wetter. The razor-sharp Ko'olau Mountain Range splits the island in two. When the trade winds blow in off the ocean and run into the vertical cliffs of the Ko'olaus, the wind is forced upward. The heavy moisture-laden clouds then build up on the ridgeline and dump a high volume of precipitation on and around the mountains.

Periodically, throughout the year, the winds will shift from the easterly trades and come in from the southwest. The southwesterly winds, also known as "Kona winds," bring in warm, moist air from the south, but they also bring in sulfur fumes from the active volcanoes on the Big Island of Hawai'i. Kona conditions cause a smoggy build-up, known as "vog" (volcanic smog). If you have allergies or suffer from respiratory ailments, you should avoid excessive activities during Kona wind periods.

When running in any tropical climate, be sure to take in fluids before, during, and after your run. The public parks on O'ahu offer rest rooms and water fountains, and an abundance of 24-hour mini-marts offer a wide selection of water and sports drinks in almost every neighborhood. Plus, the tropical sun in Hawai'i is quite strong.

The cooling trade winds can mask the burning effect, so be sure to use a waterproof sunblock while you are running to avoid burning.

O'ahu is the most heavily populated island in the Hawaiian chain, with approximately 876,000 people. In addition to the resident population, O'ahu is also the home for 34,000 active military and 50,000 military dependents, not to mention an average of 400,000 visitors a year. Most of O'ahu's residents are concentrated in the Honolulu and central O'ahu regions. Pearl City and 'Aiea are also quite congested areas with very heavy traffic and few safe running routes. One major problem faced by runners on O'ahu is the fact that close to 800,000 registered vehicles are on the island, with a limited number of roads. This combination results in congested roadways, so the search for safe and secluded running routes can be a challenge.

Despite some crowded neighborhoods and traffic jams, O'ahu is a wonderful place to enjoy the outdoors, and much of the population is active and healthy. Road races, triathlons, bike events, and a wide range of ocean competitions are extremely well attended and available on a weekly basis throughout the entire year. As a result, O'ahu boasts the highest life expectancy in the country.

RUNNING ON TRAILS Trail-running provides a great change of pace from running on the roads and also helps to develop and strengthen many of the smaller muscles and tendons in your legs. Trails offer softer surfaces, reducing the pounding on your legs. Runners often prefer trail-running as a way to escape the crowds, noise, and heavy traffic. Most of O'ahu's many trails are through dense forests, which offer a welcome break from the harsh summer sun.

However, you should choose your trails carefully. Some of the trails are simply not conducive to running, whether it is because of their slippery conditions, steep grades, or hazardous drop-offs. Many of the popular trails are located along the mountain ridges, and the rock base of O'ahu's mountains is volcanic lava. As a result, the near-vertical cliffs are unstable, and excessively dry periods or heavy rains can cause landslides. After you choose a trail for your next run, go with someone familiar with the trail, or even plan to walk the trail first. Avoid running trails alone, and be sure to inform a friend where you will be running and when you expect to return.

Also, use trail-specific running shoes. Trail shoes have thicker soles that protect your feet from sharp stones and needles, along with reinforced bumpers on the front that will reduce the shock to your toes if you stub your foot on a rock or tree root. These shoes also have an extensive sole pattern that provides greater traction on slippery surfaces.

This book lists only a few trail courses that are recommended due to their compatibility with runners and high level of maintenance. The State Department of Land and Natural Resources maintains a series of approximately forty trails that are free and open to the public. You can obtain maps and descriptions of these trails through the department's Forestry and Wildlife Division, or on their web site at *www.hawaiitrails.org*. When selecting a trail, be sure it is open to the public. Some excellent trails are located on private property and require special permission. Check with the landowners before using their trails.

Wildlife that you may encounter on trails is limited primarily to wild pigs and mongoose. Neither of these is much of a threat, as they will try to avoid humans as much as possible. On a rare occasion when a wild pig feels cornered or is protecting its young, it has been known to charge a human. O'ahu is free of poisonous snakes and other dangerous reptiles, but centipedes and a variety of bees will sting and can cause problems to those who suffer from allergic reactions.

A variety of tropical plants thrive throughout O'ahu's rain forests, but the islands are thankfully free of those nasty poisonous ivies, oaks, and sumac that can cause so much discomfort to the unobservant runner on the mainland. Many kinds of edible fruit grow in the wild along the trails and can provide a nice treat. Strawberry guavas and mountain apples are quite common, but do not try any fruit that is unfamiliar.

Finally, trail preservation is a big concern. O'ahu's trail system is quite fragile. Heavy rains and the porous lava rock base make for brittle surfaces susceptible to erosion. Stay on the marked trail at all times to avoid damaging the environment.

RUNNING ROUTES When planning this book, I wanted to identify a variety of routes that would incorporate short, medium, and long runs, as well as specialty routes designed for hill training or speed work. I also felt a need to include some trail runs for a change of pace. The challenge was limiting the number of courses to a manageable amount while trying to include all geographic regions of O'ahu. For my final selection, I created a basic formula of what specific requirements each route had to meet in order to be included.

First, each route needed to have accessible parking. Second, the routes had to cross very few, if any, major intersections. Third, public rest rooms and water fountains had to be accessible either at the start and finish or at least somewhere along the route. I did include some trail runs and very easily could have listed quite a few more, but I selected these particular routes because these trails allow you to maintain a steady pace throughout, are quite safe, and are extremely well maintained. The St. Louis Heights Trail is an exception. It is very steep and not especially safe thanks to the number of downhill bikers who frequent this trail. However, I included this particular trail because it offers a great hill-training run for advanced runners only. For a more complete guide to the trails of O'ahu, I recommend *Mountain Biking the Hawaiian Islands*, by John Alford, *The Hikers Guide to O'ahu*, by Stuart M. Ball, and the State Department of Land and Natural Resources' web site at *www.hawaiitrails.org*.

For each course described in this book, I have provided a personal rating chart that grades the courses in the following areas: course quality, parking, amenities, and safety. The explanation of my ratings is as follows (the "standards" used are based on my own personal opinion):

朮 朮 朮 朮 朮	*Exceptional. The highest level. Exceeds all standards.*
朮 朮 朮 朮	*Very good. Generally exceeds standards.*
朮 朮 朮	*Satisfactory. Acceptable. Meets the high standards one expects to find in Hawai'i.*
朮 朮	*Fair. Adequate. Meets some, but not all, standards.*
朮	*Unsatisfactory. Inadequate and substandard. Generally fails to meet the standards.*

For the Overall Course Rating, the following descriptions should be added to the explanations listed above.

🏄 🏄 🏄 🏄 🏄   *Exceptional. Heaven on earth. So wonderful you will remember it well 15 years later.*

🏄 🏄 🏄 🏄   *Very good. After completing your run, you will feel that the experience made your day. And, 10 years later, you will still feel the same way.*

🏄 🏄 🏄   *Satisfactory. You will probably return to the course every so often when you are looking for variation.*

🏄 🏄   *Fair. Pretty good, but a few things make the experience less than you would hope for.*

🏄   *Unsatisfactory. At least you were able to exercise. Let's face it, how bad can it be? You are in Hawai'i!*

RUNNING ROUTES SUMMARY TABLE

COURSE	REGION	DISTANCE MILES (KM)	TRAINING OR LENGTH	SURFACE	WATER	REST ROOMS	BEACH ACCESS
ʻAiea Loop Trail	8	4.5 (7.24)	Off-road	Dirt trail; exposed roots; hilly	Yes	Yes	No
ʻAikahi and Kāneʻohe Bay Loop	3	4.8 (7.72)	Medium	Blacktop and sidewalk; hilly	Yes	Yes	No
Ala Moana Beach Park and Magic Island	1	1.9/2.6 (3.06/4.18)	Medium	Sidewalks and blacktop walkways; flat	Yes	Yes	Yes
Ala Wai Loop	1	3.6 (5.8)	Medium	Sidewalks and bike path; flat	Yes	Yes	No
College Hill Loop	1	0.4 (640 m)	Speed training	Blacktop; hilly	No	No	No
Diamond Head	1	4.5/6.2 (7.24/10)	Medium	Blacktop; hilly	Yes	Yes	Yes
Diamond Head Hill Training	1	1 (1.61)	Speed training	Blacktop; hilly	Yes	Yes	Yes
Enchanted Lakes Loop	3	2.9/6.1 (4.67/9.82)	Medium	Sidewalks and blacktop; flat	Yes	Yes	No
ʻEwa and Barber's Point (Kalaeloa)	8	9.6 (15.45)	Long	Blacktop; wide crushed coral shoulders	Yes	Yes	No
ʻEwa and West Loch Bike Path	8	4 (6.44)	Short to medium	Bike path	Yes	Yes	No
ʻEwa and White Sands Beach	8	9 (14.49)*	Long	Blacktop; wide crushed coral shoulders	Yes	Yes	Yes
Haleʻiwa to Kuilima	5	8/22.4 (12.88/36.06)*	Long	Blacktop; mostly flat	Yes	Yes	Yes
Haleʻiwa and Waialua Loops	5	4.1/6.5/10.7 (6.6/10.46/17.22)	Medium to long	Blacktop; flat	Yes	Yes	Yes

*Distance out-and-back.

RUNNING ROUTES SUMMARY TABLE, *Continued*

COURSE	REGION	DISTANCE MILES (KM)	TRAINING OR LENGTH	SURFACE	WATER	REST ROOMS	BEACH ACCESS
Hawai'i Convention Center and Ala Wai Canal	1	0.35 (560 m)	Speed training	Brick walkway and cement sidewalks; flat	Yes	Yes	No
Hawai'i Kai Loops	2	1.4/2.37/4/4.71 (2.25/3.81/6.44/7.58)	Medium	Blacktop and some sidewalks; flat	Yes	Yes	Yes
Ho'omaluhia Botanical Garden and Old Pali Road	3	5/8.7 (8.05/14)	Medium to long	Blacktop; hilly	Yes	Yes	No
Kāhala Loops	1	3.86/4.38 (6.21/7.05)	Medium	Blacktop and some sidewalks; hilly	Yes	Yes	Yes
Kāhala (Triangle Park) to Hawai'i Kai	1, 2	Up to 18 (29)*	Medium to long	Blacktop and sidewalks; flat	Yes	Yes	Yes
Kahana to Kuilima	4	3.7/27.4 (5.95/44.1)*	Medium to long	Blacktop and coastline road; relatively flat	Yes	Yes	Yes
Kailua Beach Loops	3	4/7/10/13 (6.44/11.27/16.1/20.93)	Medium to long	Sand, blacktop, sidewalks, and bike paths; flat	Yes	Yes	Yes
Kapi'olani Community College Loop	1	1.26 (2.03)	Hill or speed training	Sidewalks; steep hills	Yes	No	No
Kapi'olani Park	1	1.85/2.2 (2.98/3.54)	Short	Blacktop and sidewalks; flat	Yes	Yes	Yes
Kapi'olani Park to Aloha Tower	1	Up to 13.36 (21.5)*	Short to long	Blacktop and cement sidewalks; a short stretch of sand; flat	Yes	Yes	Yes
Kualoa Beach Park to Punalu'u Beach Park	4	5.2/13.5 (8.37/21.73)*	Long	Blacktop and coastline road; relatively flat	Yes	Yes	Yes

Lanikai Loop	3	2.45 (3.94)	Medium	Blacktop and bike path; flat, with gentle hills	Yes	Yes	Yes
Mākaha to Yokohama Bay	6	Up to 10.56 (17)*	Medium to long	Blacktop and cement sidewalks; flat	Yes	Yes	Yes
Mānoa Valley	1	3.1/5.18 (5/8.34)	Medium	Blacktop; some grass shoulders; gentle hills	Yes	Yes	No
Mililani Town and Mililani Mauka	7	5/6.6/9.2 (8.05/10.62/14.81)	Medium to long	Sidewalks; hilly	Yes	Yes	No
Mokulēʻia to Kaʻena Point	5	5.6/15.6 (9.01/25.1)*	Medium to long	Blacktop; sand and rock trail	Yes	Yes	Yes
Pali and Maunawili Trail	3	Up to 10 (16.1)	Medium to long	Trail; moderate to steep hills	No	No	No
Pearl City Bike Path	8	5.85/11.7 (9.41/18.83)*	Medium	Blacktop; mostly flat	Yes	Yes	No
South Shore Loop	2	7/12 (11.27/19.31)	Medium to long	Blacktop; rolling hills	Yes	Yes	Yes
St. Louis Heights Trail	1	1.5 (2.42)	Medium and hill training	Trail; very rugged and steep	Yes	Yes	No
Tantalus Loop	1	10 (16.1)	Long and hill training	Blacktop; very hilly	Yes	Yes	No
Tantalus Trails	1	Varies	Medium to long	Trails; very hilly	No	No	No
Temple Valley and Kāneʻohe Bay	3	8.2 (13.2)	Medium	Blacktop; rolling hills	Yes	Yes	Yes

Distance out-and-back.

HONOLULU

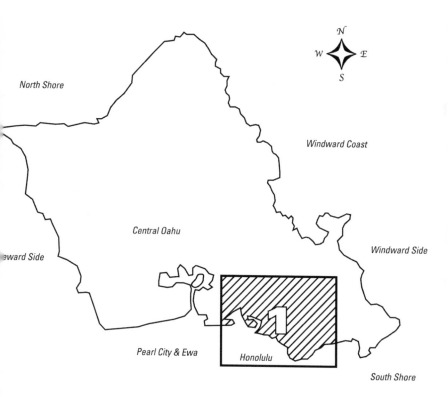

North Shore

Windward Coast

Central Oahu

Windward Side

eward Side

Pearl City & Ewa

Honolulu

South Shore

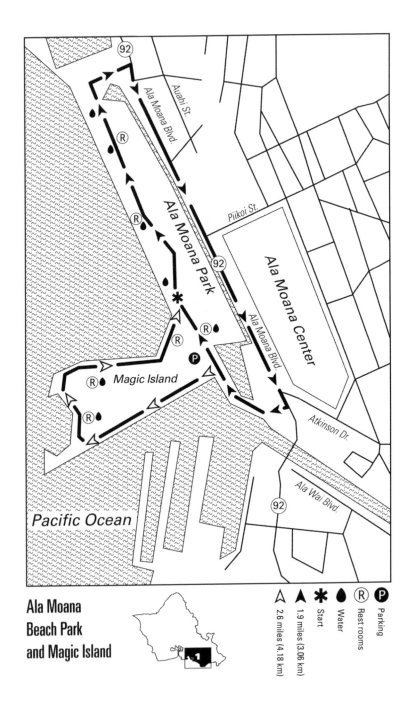

Ala Moana
Beach Park
and Magic Island

Pacific Ocean

Ala Moana Blvd.

Auahi St.

Ala Moana Park

Piikoi St.

Ala Moana Center

Ala Moana Blvd.

Atkinson Dr.

Ala Wai Blvd.

Magic Island

2.6 miles (4.18 km)

1.9 miles (3.06 km)

Start

Water

Rest rooms

Parking

ALA MOANA BEACH PARK AND MAGIC ISLAND

DISTANCE:	*1.9 miles or 2.6 miles with Magic Island (3.06 or 4.18 km)*
SURFACE:	*Sidewalks and blacktop walkways; flat*
SUITABLE FOR:	*All levels*
LOCATION:	*Honolulu (Map Region 1)*
PARK HOURS:	*Parking area closes at 10:00 PM nightly.*
COURSE:	🏃 🏃 🏃
PARKING:	🏃 🏃 🏃 🏃 🏃
AMENITIES:	🏃 🏃 🏃 🏃 🏃
SAFETY:	🏃 🏃 🏃 🏃
OVERALL RATING:	🏃 🏃 🏃 🏃

OVERVIEW Ala Moana Beach Park is one of the most popular beach parks on O'ahu. Seven days a week this 76-acre park is packed with sun worshippers, surfers, picnickers, skate boarders, runners, and a multitude of others. First developed in 1934, this man-made beach now boasts an 0.5-mile-long lagoon, perfect for safe water recreation and long training swims. In 1998, Honolulu city and county completed a massive overhaul of the park, improving the sidewalks, water fountains, two refreshment stands, and rest room facilities. They also added lighting along the perimeter sidewalks, which provides safety for night runs.

One major reason for Ala Moana's popularity is the weather. This spot is one of the sunniest on O'ahu. The downside of that distinction is it can become quite hot during the day. Even though you can see runners at all hours of the day, the majority of them prefer early mornings and late afternoons. This is a tremendous place to run while watching the sun set. The parking lots at Ala Moana close at 10:00 PM, but the good lighting makes this location popular and relatively safe for night runs.

Another benefit of running at Ala Moana is the park's excellent swimming lagoon. For those who prefer to diversify their training, there is nothing better than taking a refreshing swim after a long, hot run. Ala Moana's protective reef shelters swimmers from the high surf, dangerous currents, and, of course, hungry sharks who might mistake you for a juicy sea turtle.

DIRECTIONS Located between downtown Honolulu and Waikīkī, the beach park is across the street from the Ala Moana Shopping Center. Enter the park off Ala Moana Boulevard. Parking may be difficult on the weekends and holidays, unless you come early.

COURSE Starting at the end of the park nearest Diamond Head and Waikīkī, you can choose to run in either direction around the perimeter of the park. By following the perimeter sidewalk, the run will be 1.9 miles per loop. Add Magic Island to your run, and the loop is extended to 2.5 miles. This flat course is primarily on sidewalks, but the section through Magic Island is blacktop. All along the beach side of the loop, you will find numerous water fountains, four rest room facilities (six if you include Magic Island), an exercise unit, two refreshment stands, and at least a dozen showers. It does not get any easier than this.

HIGHLIGHTS Quite a few surfing competitions are held beyond Ala Moana's reef, mostly during the summer months. Ala Moana is also the site for biathlons and triathlons, and it hosts several cultural and sports activities throughout the year. Magic Island was created in 1964, when developers used coral and sand dredged from the construction of the Ala Wai Boat Harbor to create this peninsula, which was to be the first phase of a major resort hotel complex. Fortunately, the developers ran into financial trouble, and the peninsula was converted to a popular public park that now serves as a beautiful border to Waikīkī. In 2001, an extensive beautification project was completed, and a large number of trees were added to the Magic Island landscape. One of the arborists who took a leadership role pushing for the planting of the additional trees was Christine Snyder of Kailua. Tragically, Christine lost her life in the September 11 terrorist attacks. A tree was planted in her honor along the jogging trail portion of Magic Island. The Ala Moana Beach Park was also a man-made beach. Before it was developed, this entire park area was nothing more than a swamp, and the shoreline was a combination of coral and mud flats. The actual swimming area was originally cleared to serve as a boat channel to join the Kewalo Basin with the Ala Wai Canal. It was not until 1955 that the 'Ewa end of the channel was closed off and sand was brought in from north shore beaches to cover the coral fill and create this popular beach.

CAUTIONS   Because this park is often full of people, you will have to share the running paths with numerous in-line skaters and walkers. This park is heavily patrolled by the Honolulu Police Department, and lifeguard stands are every 200 meters along the beach. The water at Ala Moana is extremely safe for swimmers of all levels, and it is hard to resist a nice plunge in the water after a hard run. Since you probably will be tempted by the water, be careful about the periodic invasion of box jellyfish. These particular jellyfish appear only for a few days following a full moon. Check with the lifeguards, and they can tell you exactly when the next box jellyfish invasion will take place.

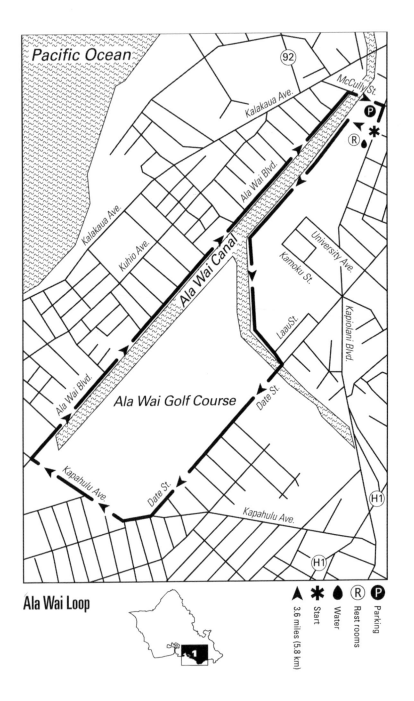

Pacific Ocean

92

McCully St.

Kalakaua Ave.

P

R

*

Ala Wai Blvd.

Kalakaua Ave.

University Ave.

Kuhio Ave.

Kamoku St.

Ala Wai Canal

Laau St.

Kapiolani Blvd.

Ala Wai Blvd.

Ala Wai Golf Course

Date St.

Kapahulu Ave.

Date St.

H1

Kapahulu Ave.

H1

Ala Wai Loop

1

N

* Start

Water

R Rest rooms

P Parking

3.6 miles (5.8 km)

ALA WAI LOOP

DISTANCE:	*3.6 miles (5.8 km)*
SURFACE:	*Sidewalks and bike path; flat*
SUITABLE FOR:	*All levels*
LOCATION:	*Honolulu (Map Region 1)*
COURSE:	🏃 🏃 🏃 🏃
PARKING:	🏃 🏃
AMENITIES:	🏃 🏃
SAFETY:	🏃 🏃 🏃 🏃
OVERALL RATING:	🏃 🏃 🏃

OVERVIEW This 3.6-mile loop is convenient to all the Waikīkī hotels and provides a safe, flat course with only one intersection crossing. The Ala Wai loop is a popular walking route and can get congested in the early evenings, but you can get your mileage in without having to deal with traffic.

DIRECTIONS From any of the Waikīkī hotels, simply walk one or two blocks *mauka* (toward the mountains), and you will come to the Ala Wai Boulevard. Cross the boulevard, and start anywhere along the sidewalk edging the canal. From downtown, leeward or windward, take H1 east. Take the King Street exit, and continue straight to the second traffic light. Turn right on Kapahulu Avenue. Follow Kapahulu for about 1 mile, turning right on Ala Wai Boulevard. After 5:30 PM street parking is free along the Ala Wai. Other free parking options include the Ala Wai Field Park across the McCully Street Bridge on the opposite side of the canal from Waikīkī and Kapiʻolani Park just off Monsarrat Avenue, next to the Waikīkī Bandstand and the Waikīkī Shell. The last lot is about 0.5 mile from the Ala Wai loop. From east Honolulu, take H1 west. Exit at Kapiʻolani Boulevard. Follow Kapiʻolani Boulevard, staying in the left lane. Take a left on McCully, and cross the Ala Wai Canal. After a block, McCully merges with Kalākaua Avenue. If you plan to park at Kapiʻolani Park, take Kalākaua to Kapahulu. Just past Kapahulu, you will come to a "Y"; stay to the left on Monsarrat, and the parking area will be on your right.

COURSE Start at any point along the Ala Wai Canal heading away from Diamond Head. Continue along the sidewalk bordering the canal. At the McCully Street Bridge, turn right over the bridge. At Kapiʻolani Boulevard, turn right, and immediately turn right again into the parking lot of the Ala Wai Field, which is the starting point designated on the map. Continue through the parking lot past the baseball field on your left. As you reach the canal, take a left at the start of the bike path that will take you in the Diamond Head direction along the canal, opposite Waikīkī. This section can get crowded, as it is the site where a number of paddling clubs house their canoes. Follow the bike path past the Ala Wai Elementary School and the ʻIolani High School track. Just past the track, the path bends to the left and follows the Mānoa Flood Canal for a short stretch. Turn right at Date Street, and run along the Ala Wai Golf Course. At the end of the golf course and just prior to Kapahulu Avenue, the path turns right. Continue on the bike path along Kapahulu Avenue. After you pass the Ala Wai Public Library, turn right on Ala Wai Boulevard to complete the loop.

HIGHLIGHTS Prior to the construction of the Ala Wai Canal in the 1920s, Waikīkī had been mostly unsanitary swamps and duck ponds with serious mosquito problems. The canal was created to pull the water out of Waikīkī to create a solid base for the development of what has now become one of the most recognized tourist destinations in the world. In Hawaiian, "*ala wai*" means "freshwater way," although today it is anything but. Runoff from tributary streams and a buildup of silt have caused some pollution problems with the canal. Swimming is strongly discouraged, but the canal is often used as a popular training location for paddlers and kayakers. Founded in 1836, ʻIolani High School is one of the finest private schools in Hawaiʻi. The Ala Wai Golf Course is the only urban golf course in Hawaiʻi and is also the busiest public golf course in the world, averaging over 175,000 rounds of golf a year.

CAUTIONS Be especially careful crossing Ala Wai Boulevard. Although a one-way road, it is the main traffic artery out of Waikīkī, and traffic can get heavy. During the evening hours, the sidewalk bordering the Waikīkī side of the canal is well-lit, but the bike path on the opposite side is dark in areas. The sidewalk on the Waikīkī side of the canal is often traveled by walkers and joggers moving in both directions, so take caution.

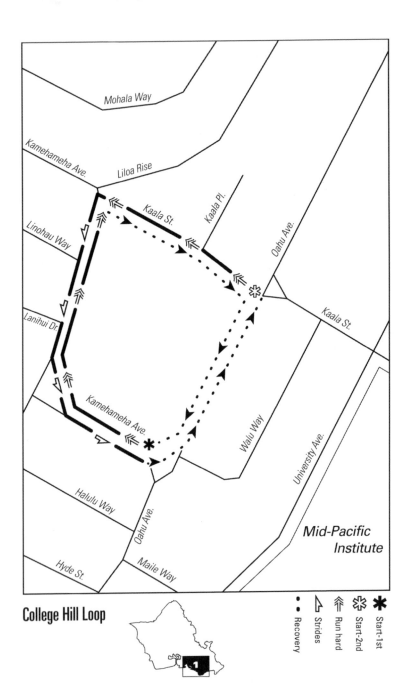

Mohala Way

Kamehameha Ave.

Liloa Rise

Kaala St.

Kaala Pl.

Oahu Ave.

Linohau Way

Kaala St.

Lanihui Dr.

Kamehameha Ave.

Walu Way

University Ave.

Halulu Way

Oahu Ave.

Mid-Pacific
Institute

Hyde St.

Maile Way

College Hill Loop

⋮ Recovery

▷ Strides

⇑ Run hard

✳ Start-2nd

✸ Start-1st

COLLEGE HILL LOOP

DISTANCE:	*0.4 mile (640 meters)*
SURFACE:	*Blacktop; hilly*
SUITABLE FOR:	*Intermediate to advanced; speed training*
LOCATION:	*Honolulu (Map Region 1)*
COURSE:	🏃 🏃 🏃 🏃
PARKING:	🏃 🏃
AMENITIES:	🏃
SAFETY:	🏃 🏃 🏃
OVERALL RATING:	🏃 🏃 🏃

OVERVIEW The course is a one-block loop around the University of Hawai'i president's home, also known as College Hill. This loop is good for training because it offers different types of speed or hill training, depending on whether you run clockwise or counterclockwise. This loop is very short, so be sure to combine it with sufficient warm-up and warm-down runs.

DIRECTIONS From H1 east or west, take the University exit, and follow University Avenue past the University of Hawai'i. At the top of the hill (at the third traffic light), turn left on Maile Way. Take a right at the stop sign, and find some street parking close to the next intersection of O'ahu Avenue and Kamehameha Avenue. This corner is the start of the loop. During the school year, parking is very limited in this neighborhood, so you may choose to continue along O'ahu Avenue for about 1 mile. Parking becomes easier the farther you get from the university. This option can also ensure that you do the recommended warm-up and warm-down runs.

COURSE You have no chance of getting lost on this course. Starting at the corner of O'ahu Avenue and Kamehameha Avenue, run at race pace up Kamehameha Avenue for one block. The road bends to the right. Continue at race pace up Kamehameha Avenue for one more block to the one-way sign at Ka'ala, which is the end of the first portion of your run. Turn right on Ka'ala, and do a recovery jog or walk to the bottom of the hill. Turn right on O'ahu Avenue, and head back to the starting point.

If you run in this manner, you will find that the Kamehameha Avenue stretch offers a slight uphill with the grade becoming progressively steeper as you near the Ka'ala intersection. This provides the feel of running 200-meter repeats with a hill. Repeat this loop five to ten times for a great workout. To get a completely different feel, turn around, and run the loop in a counterclockwise direction. Starting at the corner of O'ahu and Ka'ala, run hard up Ka'ala. Pump your arms hard, lift your knees high, and keep the stride short. Don't let up at the top of the hill. Take the left onto Kamehameha Avenue, and accelerate down the gentle hill using exaggerated, elongated strides. At O'ahu Avenue, slow to a jog or walk, and use O'ahu Avenue as a recovery before repeating the sprint up Ka'ala. Repeat five to ten times. To get a well-rounded training session, complete five loops clockwise and five loops counterclockwise.

HIGHLIGHTS This loop takes you around the historic College Hill. Built in the early 1900s by Frank C. Atherton, this stately home was given to the University of Hawai'i in 1963 to serve as the university president's residence. College Hill has undergone numerous facelifts since 1963 and has been home for six different presidents and their families.

CAUTIONS Despite its appearance as a peaceful and quiet neighborhood, the close proximity to the university assures a steady flow of traffic and limited parking along O'ahu and Kamehameha Avenue. Run defensively. Many drivers in this area are aggressively searching for parking and do not always take notice of runners. Although there are streetlights, the heavy tree cover reduces their effectiveness, leaving these streets rather dark after sundown. No public rest rooms are in the near proximity, so unless you have the nerve to knock on the president's door, be sure to take care of business before you start.

DIAMOND HEAD

DISTANCE:	*4.5 or 6.2 miles (7.24 or 10 km)*
SURFACE:	*Blacktop; hilly*
SUITABLE FOR:	*All levels*
LOCATION:	*Honolulu (Map Region 1)*
COURSE:	🏃 🏃 🏃 🏃
PARKING:	🏃 🏃 🏃 🏃
AMENITIES:	🏃 🏃 🏃 🏃
SAFETY:	🏃 🏃 🏃 🏃 🏃
OVERALL RATING:	🏃 🏃 🏃 🏃

OVERVIEW This course is popular with runners of all levels because of its easy access and ample parking. The loops that include Diamond Head are also excellent for hill training. Rest rooms and water fountains are located throughout Kapiʻolani Park. Water is also available at the top of Monsarrat in front of the little white church and at the top of the hill fronting Diamond Head close to the lighthouse. The number of runners along this route grows dramatically prior to major local races, such as the Great Aloha Run, the Honolulu Marathon, and the Tinman Triathlon.

DIRECTIONS From downtown or beyond, take H1 east, and exit at King Street. Continue straight through the traffic light, and turn right on Kapahulu Avenue. Continue to the end of Kapahulu, then turn left. When the road splits, bear to the left. Make the first right into the free parking lot next to the Waikīkī Bandstand. From east Honolulu, take Kalanianaʻole Highway, and exit at Waiʻalae Avenue. Take a left at the first traffic light on Kīlauea Avenue. After four traffic lights, take the next left on ʻElepaio. At the end of ʻElepaio, turn right on Kāhala Avenue. After passing Fort Ruger Park (better known in the running community as Triangle Park), Kāhala Avenue becomes Diamond Head Road. Continue straight around the front of Diamond Head. At the stop sign, bear to the left down Kalākaua Avenue. At the end of the park, Kalākaua takes a sharp

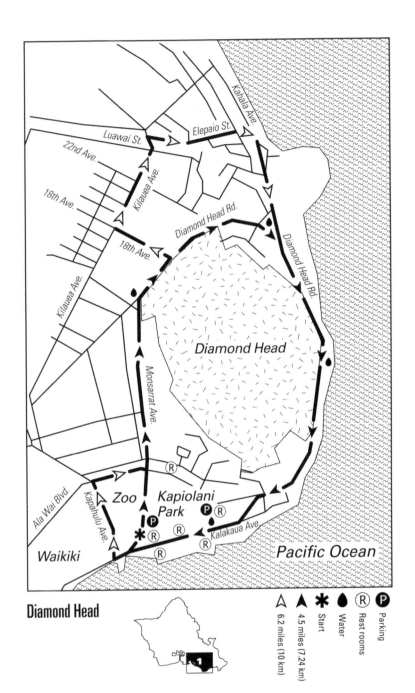

Diamond Head

Luawai St.
Elepaio St.
Kahala Ave.
22nd Ave.
Kilauea Ave.
18th Ave.
18th Ave.
Diamond Head Rd.
Diamond Head Rd.
Kilauea Ave.

Diamond Head

Monsarrat Ave.

Ala Wai Blvd.
Zoo
Kapiolani Park
R
P
R
R
R
R
R
R
Kapahulu Ave.
Waikiki
Kalakaua Ave.

Pacific Ocean

1

6.2 miles (10 km)
4.5 miles (7.24 km)
Start
Water
R Rest rooms
P Parking

right and becomes Monsarrat Avenue. Make an immediate right into the bandstand parking area.

COURSE The loop around Diamond Head is 4.5 miles. Start at the Waikīkī Bandstand, which is an excellent meeting place with rest rooms, water fountains, and plenty of free parking. From here you have a number of choices—you can run the loop either clockwise or counterclockwise. Clockwise is rated more difficult, but both directions provide substantial hill climbs. If running clockwise, head directly up Monsarrat Avenue. Monsarrat soon becomes a long, mildly steep climb. At the top of the hill, Monsarrat Avenue becomes Diamond Head Road and starts a gentle decline down along the back side of Diamond Head. Continue around Diamond Head, running along the coast, past the lighthouse, down to sea level, and back into Kapiʻolani Park, where you will take a left on Kalākaua Avenue. This part of the course is the final stretch of the Honolulu Marathon, so picture yourself having completed 25 miles, entering the park with thousands of people cheering you on.

To increase the run to 6.2 miles, start at the bandstand, but, instead of heading straight up Monsarrat, head out, and run clockwise around the Honolulu Zoo. When you get back to Monsarrat, turn left up the Monsarrat hill. After the summit, take the first left on 18th Avenue. Continue on 18th for one block, then turn right on Kīlauea Avenue, and run down Kīlauea for 0.5 mile. Turn right on ʻElepaio, and follow ʻElepaio until it ends at Kāhala Avenue. Turn right on Kāhala, and follow this road straight up over Diamond Head and then down into Kapiʻolani Park, finishing in front of the Waikīkī Bandstand.

HIGHLIGHTS As mentioned, this route is a favorite among runners, so you never know whom you will run into along the way. If it's close to the time of the Honolulu Marathon, you might spot some of the unbelievable Kenyan runners blazing by. The surf at Diamond Head Beach is world-renowned for windsurfing, so if the wind and surf conditions are right, keep an eye out for one of the professional windsurfing competitions. As you run along the stone wall facing Diamond Head Beach, also check out the beautiful gardens planted along the edge of the cliff. Some of the old-time surfers who frequent this surf spot planted and maintained these gardens. After your run, cross over Kalākaua, and take a refreshing dip at Kaimana Beach, located to the left of the Natatorium. Kapiʻolani Park also houses the Waikīkī Shell, where evening concerts are held throughout the year. Across from the tennis courts are the Waikīkī Aquarium and the Natatorium War Memorial, which was built to honor veterans of World War I. After a short run and a refreshing swim, go back across Kalākaua, and check out the Honolulu Zoo.

CAUTIONS You will have very few intersections to cross, but please be careful. Drivers are often so busy taking in the sights that they sometimes fail to notice runners, so it is up to you to run defensively. Cyclists also like this route, so be courteous. The parking area is free, but it fills up fast, so get there early. If the lot is full, metered parking is along Kalākaua Avenue, and some additional free parking is on the mountain, or *mauka*, side of the park. This busy park is well patrolled by police, but it is always good practice not to leave any valuables in your car.

DIAMOND HEAD HILL TRAINING

DISTANCE:	*1-mile repeats (1.61 km)*
SURFACE:	*Blacktop; hilly*
SUITABLE FOR:	*Intermediate to advanced; hill and speed training*
LOCATION:	*Honolulu (Map Region 1)*
COURSE:	🏃 🏃 🏃 🏃 🏃
PARKING:	🏃 🏃 🏃 🏃
AMENITIES:	🏃 🏃 🏃 🏃
SAFETY:	🏃 🏃 🏃
OVERALL RATING:	🏃 🏃 🏃 🏃

OVERVIEW The majestic Diamond Head serves as the tremendous backdrop to this challenging training course. Diamond Head Road runs above the rugged coastline around the southern edge of Diamond Head. Parking is available at the base of Diamond Head in Kapi'olani Park. The park also offers numerous public rest rooms and water fountains.

DIRECTIONS The starting point for this run is Kapi'olani Park. To get to the park from windward or west O'ahu, take H1 east to the King Street exit. Continue to the second traffic light, and turn right on Kapahulu Avenue. Kapahulu ends at Waikīkī Beach. At this point, take a left, and bear to the left at the "Y" in front of the Honolulu Zoo. A large, free parking lot will be on your right.

From east Honolulu, take H1 west to the Kapi'olani Boulevard exit. Once on Kapi'olani Boulevard, move to the far-left lane, and turn left on McCully. After crossing the Ala Wai Canal and Ala Wai Boulevard, turn left on Kalākaua Avenue, and continue through Waikīkī. In front of the Honolulu Zoo, stay to the left on Monsarrat, and take the first right into the free parking lot in front of the Waikīkī Bandstand in Kapi'olani Park.

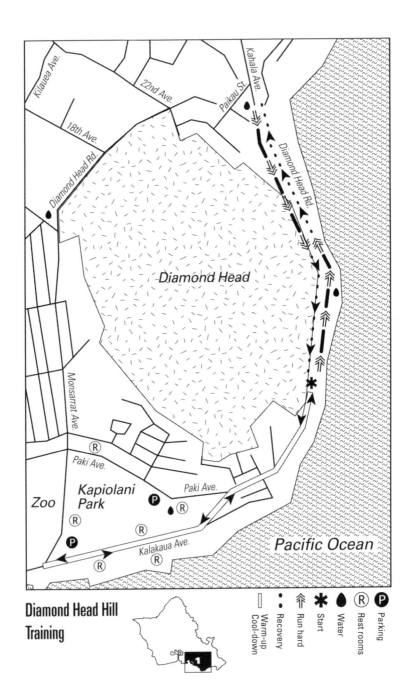

Diamond Head Hill Training

Kīlauea Ave.

22nd Ave.

18th Ave.

Paikau St.

Kahala Ave.

Diamond Head Rd.

Diamond Head Rd.

Diamond Head

Monsarrat Ave.

Paki Ave.

Paki Ave.

Zoo

Kapiolani Park

(R)

(P)

(R)

(R)

(R)

(P)

(R)

Kalakaua Ave.

(R)

Pacific Ocean

Warm-up Cool-down

Recovery

Run hard

Start

Water

(R) Rest rooms

(P) Parking

COURSE A good starting point is the Waikīkī Bandstand in Kapiʻolani Park. From the bandstand, run one loop of the park to give yourself a proper warm-up. After the loop, exit the park at the south end following Diamond Head Road. Stop at the point where the grade of the road becomes steeper, and this will be the starting point for the first hill run. Begin up the steep grade at race pace. The road levels somewhat after the lighthouse, but continue at race pace until you come to a stone monument located in a parking area on the right. At the monument, slow your pace to either a walk or a slow recovery jog. Continue along Diamond Head Road until you reach Fort Ruger Park (known by most residents as Triangle Park), which is the end of your recovery. At this point, turn around and head back up Diamond Head Road at race pace until you reach the same stone monument. Again, slow to a walk or jog, and continue to the original starting point.

Each of these hard runs is 0.5-mile in length with a 0.5-mile recovery. The beauty of this hill training is that the first hill is a much steeper grade but levels off within 0.25 mile. The second hill offers a gentler grade, but the grade continues for the entire 0.5 mile. The steeper grade requires shorter strides and helps develop strong upward thrusting knee lifts. The milder grade allows for longer, more fluid strides. Repeat each run three to six times before commencing a warm-down jog back to Kapiʻolani Park.

HIGHLIGHTS The natural beauty of this stretch of road is breathtaking (as if racing up its steep grade isn't breathtaking enough). The cooler late afternoon or early evening hours are a popular time for this particular training session, and these times also offer some spectacular sunset-viewing opportunities. The ocean break off Diamond Head Beach is a favorite spot for both surfers and windsurfers. This stretch of Diamond Head Road constitutes the only real hills of the Honolulu Marathon (mile 8 on the way out, and mile 24.5 on the way back).

CAUTIONS This section of road is often full of tour buses and sightseers. In other words, run defensively. So many things to see are along this stretch that runners are usually the last thing on people's minds. Stay alert for cars backing out of the parking areas and for surfers loading their boards onto their cars.

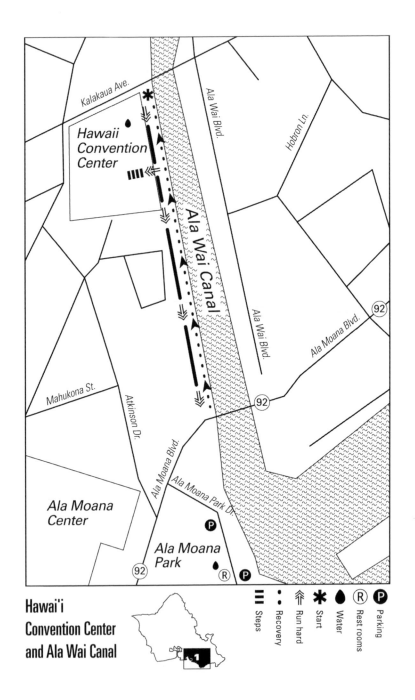

Kalakaua Ave.

Ala Wai Blvd.

Hobron Ln.

Hawaii Convention Center

Ala Wai Canal

Ala Wai Blvd.

Ala Moana Blvd.

92

Mahukona St.

Atkinson Dr.

Ala Moana Blvd.

92

Ala Moana Park Dr.

Ala Moana Center

Ala Moana Park

92

R

P

P

Hawai'i Convention Center and Ala Wai Canal

≡ Steps
⋮ Recovery
⇈ Run hard
✳ Start
⬤ Water
Ⓡ Rest rooms
🅿 Parking

HAWAI'I CONVENTION CENTER AND ALA WAI CANAL

DISTANCE:	*0.35 mile (560 meters)*
SURFACE:	*Brick walkway and cement sidewalks; flat, but with step option*
SUITABLE FOR:	*All levels; speed training*
LOCATION:	*Honolulu (Map Region 1)*
COURSE:	🏃 🏃 🏃 🏃
PARKING:	🏃 🏃 🏃 🏃
AMENITIES:	🏃 🏃 🏃
SAFETY:	🏃 🏃 🏃 🏃
OVERALL RATING:	🏃 🏃 🏃 🏃

OVERVIEW A flat, short stretch of walkway along the Ala Wai Canal fronting the Hawai'i Convention Center, this option is great for speed training if you do not have access to a track or as an alternative to the track. This wide brick walkway runs for 0.35 mile (560 meters) along the Ala Wai and is covered the entire length by beautiful shade trees. Walkers also use this area, but, under normal circumstances, the walkway is wide enough to accommodate a small group of runners without causing congestion. If you plan on using this stretch for a large group, break the group into a number of smaller groups, and send them off in 1-minute intervals.

DIRECTIONS The Hawai'i Convention Center is located at the point where Kalākaua Avenue crosses the Ala Wai Canal, within easy walking distance of Waikīkī and the Ala Moana Shopping Center. The nearby Ala Moana Beach Park offers large, free parking areas, along with ample rest room facilities and water fountains. After parking your car, complete a 1.9-mile loop of the beach park as a warm-up before continuing to the Convention Center for the speed session.

COURSE Starting at the Kalākaua Avenue end of the sidewalk, run the full length of the brick walkway at race pace. For recovery, use a light, bouncy jog along the cement sidewalk or grass area that runs the length of the canal. Repeat this loop six to ten times. To top off this speed session, finish your final recovery jog in front of the Convention Center. Here the center offers an impressive and wide set of stairs perfect for step training. After completing a few sets on the stairs, take about 10 minutes to stretch thoroughly before the final warm-down run back to and around the Ala Moana Beach Park.

HIGHLIGHTS This beautifully maintained and landscaped walkway was completed, along with the $350 million Convention Center, in 1997. The Ala Wai Canal is the training site for canoe paddling teams and kayakers, and watching these athletes returning from their open ocean training can provide a pleasant diversion. Bougainvillea also bloom all along the wall bordering the canal. This stretch of walkway is very well lit at night, so if the daytime heat is too much for you, an evening training session can be an excellent option. Late afternoon to sundown is the preferred time, for it provides milder temperatures and some spectacular sunset-viewing opportunities.

CAUTIONS Despite all the positive aspects, you should not use this stretch for your primary speed-training site. The brick surface, although attractive, is also a very hard surface, and overtraining on this type of surface can cause injuries. This site should be used as a change of pace or alternate training site. The brick surface also has a tendency to become slippery when wet, and although that should not be a problem for joggers, it can be a hazard when running hard. Heavy pedestrian traffic during major conventions can render this stretch unusable, so be sure to check with the center before adding this course to your schedule.

Furthermore, busy roads with complex intersections surround the Convention Center. Unfortunately, very few pedestrian crosswalks have been provided, so be sure to use the designated crosswalks, and be patient while waiting your turn to cross. The alternative can be quite dangerous. Getting hit by a city bus can really put a damper on a good training run.

KĀHALA LOOPS

DISTANCE:	*3.86 or 4.38 miles (6.21 or 7.05 km)*
SURFACE:	*Blacktop and some sidewalks; hilly*
SUITABLE FOR:	*All levels*
LOCATION:	*Honolulu (Map Region 1)*
COURSE:	🏃 🏃 🏃 🏃
PARKING:	🏃 🏃 🏃
AMENITIES:	🏃 🏃
SAFETY:	🏃 🏃 🏃 🏃
OVERALL RATING:	🏃 🏃 🏃 🏃

OVERVIEW For years the Kāhala neighborhood has been a favorite training site for runners. Many annual road races are run along Kāhala's shady roadways. Water is available at Triangle Park, at the Aloha gas station, and at Kaimukī Intermediate School. These two courses have some minor elevation changes, but for the most part they are flat and run on paved surfaces. Street parking is available at Triangle Park, but this park is a starting point for a number of bike clubs, so you may need to park in the surrounding neighborhood. No rest rooms are available at the park, but public rest rooms are located at the Kāhala Mall on Kīlauea Avenue.

DIRECTIONS From downtown and west Oʻahu, take H1 east, exiting at Waiʻalae Avenue. Continue on Waiʻalae, and turn right at the second traffic light onto Hunakai Street. Follow Hunakai until it ends at Kāhala Avenue. Turn right on Kāhala, and continue to the base of Diamond Head. Triangle Park is located on the right just before Kāhala Avenue becomes Diamond Head Road. Street parking is available along the southeast side of the park and in the surrounding neighborhood. As mentioned above, Triangle Park is a popular meeting place for bicyclists, so parking can be limited on weekend mornings.

From the south shore of Oʻahu, take Kalanianaʻole Highway (72) toward Honolulu. Exit at Waiʻalae Avenue, and take the first left

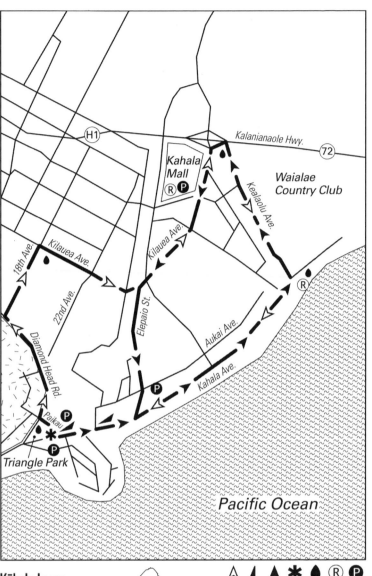

Kāhala Loops

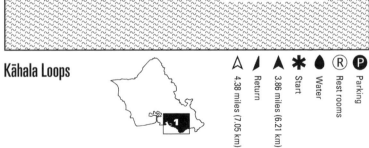

Ʌ 4.38 miles (7.05 km)	
⌐ Return	
Ʌ 3.86 miles (6.21 km)	
✳ Start	
◔ Water	
Ⓡ Rest rooms	
Ⓟ Parking	

Kahala Mall

Ⓡ Ⓟ

Waialae Country Club

Kalanianaole Hwy.

72

H1

18th Ave.

Kīlauea Ave.

22nd Ave.

Kīlauea Ave.

Kealaolu Ave.

Elepaio St.

Aukai Ave.

Diamond Head Rd.

Kahala Ave.

Ⓡ

Ⓟ

Ⓟ

Paikau

Ⓟ

✳

Triangle Park

Pacific Ocean

1

onto Kīlauea Avenue. Follow Kīlauea for just less than 1 mile, turning left on Hunakai Street. Once on Hunakai, follow the directions
described above.

COURSES For the 3.86-mile course, start from Triangle Park, and
run down Kāhala Avenue for about 1.5 miles. Turn left at the stop
sign, and follow the bike path along Kealaʻolu Avenue. At the end of
Kealaʻolu, turn left through the gas station parking area, and make
a quick left on Kīlauea. Run along the left side (facing traffic) of
Kīlauea. At the sixth intersection, ʻElepaio Street, turn left, run
down ʻElepaio until it merges into Kāhala Avenue, turn right on
Kāhala, and return to Triangle Park.

For the 4.38-mile course, head up toward Kapiʻolani Community College along Diamond Head Road. Turn right on 18th Avenue, and continue for one block before turning right on Kīlauea.
Follow Kīlauea until you reach the Kāhala Mall. Turn right through
the gas station parking area, and make another right on Kealaʻolu,
which is the 22-mile mark of the Honolulu Marathon. Continue to
the end of Kealaʻolu, and turn right on Kāhala Avenue. Follow Kāhala Avenue for a little more than 1 mile back to the starting point
at Triangle Park.

HIGHLIGHTS These loops around Kāhala are both incorporated in
the Honolulu Marathon course. Plus, the homes along Kāhala Avenue are some of the most exclusive real estate on Oʻahu. Kealaʻolu
Avenue borders the Waiʻalae Country Club, which for many years
was the site for the Hawaiian Open, now known as the PGA Tour's
Sony Open, held every January.

CAUTIONS Kāhala Avenue has no shoulder, so run facing traffic
and stay close to the curb, or run along the grass strip bordering
the road. The rest of the course offers sidewalks and fairly wide
shoulders.

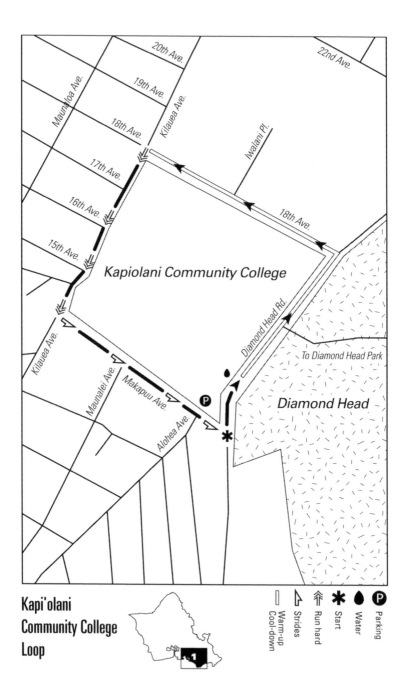

20th Ave.

22nd Ave.

19th Ave.

Maunaloa Ave.

18th Ave.

Kilauea Ave.

17th Ave.

Iwalani Pl.

16th Ave.

18th Ave.

15th Ave.

Kapiolani Community College

Kilauea Ave.

Diamond Head Rd.

To Diamond Head Park

Maunalei Ave.

Makapuu Ave.

Diamond Head

Alohea Ave.

Kapi'olani
Community College
Loop

Strides

Warm-up
Cool-down

Run hard

Start

Water

Parking

1

KAPI'OLANI COMMUNITY COLLEGE LOOP

DISTANCE:	*1.26 miles (2.03 km)*
SURFACE:	*Sidewalks; steep hills*
SUITABLE FOR:	*Advanced*
LOCATION:	*Honolulu (Map Region 1)*
COURSE:	🏃 🏃 🏃 🏃
PARKING:	🏃 🏃 🏃 🏃 🏃
AMENITIES:	🏃 🏃
SAFETY:	🏃 🏃 🏃 🏃
OVERALL RATING:	🏃 🏃 🏃 🏃

OVERVIEW Best for runners interested in getting in some intense hill training, this short loop follows the sidewalk surrounding the Kapi'olani Community College campus. Plenty of parking is available at the college on weekends and after school hours.

DIRECTIONS From Waikīkī, take Kalākaua Avenue. At the Honolulu Zoo, bear left on Monsarrat Avenue. Continue up Monsarrat to the top of the hill. Turn left at Makapu'u Avenue, then take a quick right into the Kapi'olani Community College parking lot. From Honolulu or leeward O'ahu, take H1 east. Take the Koko Head Avenue exit, and turn right on Koko Head Avenue. Continue straight through the first traffic light, and take a left on 12th Avenue. After three blocks, turn left on Alohea Avenue. Alohea will take you directly into the KCC parking lot.

COURSE Start at the corner of Makapu'u Avenue and Diamond Head Road. Turn left down Diamond Head Road, then turn left again at 18th Avenue. These two blocks will be the recovery portion of the loop. At the corner of 18th and Kīlauea Avenue, turn left, and begin your first climb. Kīlauea starts out steep, levels off for a brief moment, and then gets really steep. At the top of the hill, turn left on Makapuʻu, and stride hard down to the starting point. Turn left on Diamond Head once more, and begin your recovery jog until you get to Kīlauea again. Repeat this loop as many times as you can. The steep climb immediately followed by the gentle downhill provides the perfect combination of strength and speed training.

If you prefer a warm-up before jumping into this intense workout, park at Kapiʻolani Park, and run up to the start point. Warming up can also force you to do the necessary warm-down after this hard workout. A light, bouncy jog around Diamond Head will be perfect for ridding your body of the lactic acid that builds up during your workout.

HIGHLIGHTS As you run down Diamond Head Road, you will see a small church located on your left that belongs to the college and is used for taiko drum classes. A *taiko* is a traditional Japanese drum, and centuries ago these drums were used to call warriors to battle or, in more peaceful times, for Buddhist religious rituals. During the post–World War II period, *taiko* reemerged as a major art form in Japan and rapidly spread throughout North America. The modern-day *taiko* has blended what looks like a form of martial arts with the traditional drumming to create a dramatic and exciting display that results in an intense adrenaline rush for not only the participants but also the observers. The thundering boom of the *taiko* is like no other. A water fountain is directly in front of this church, so if the *taiko* drummers are practicing, be sure to stop for a drink and check out these artists. When you continue past the church, the road to your right leads to the Diamond Head Crater Park. Inside the crater is an extremely popular hiking trail that leads to the rim of the crater and provides the best panoramic views of Waikīkī and the south shore. After you turn left onto 18th Avenue, the facility on your left is Diamond Head Studios, which is the indoor film studio where famous television shows like *Hawaiʻi 5-0* and *Magnum P.I.* were filmed.

CAUTIONS Kīlauea Hill is extremely steep and should be run with caution. Pay attention to your body. If it starts screaming for you to slow down, slow down! Be sure you are warmed up sufficiently before you start hammering the hill, and take care to do a proper warm-down when you complete your hills.

KAPI'OLANI PARK

DISTANCE:	*1.85 or 2.2 miles (2.98 or 3.54 km)*
SURFACE:	*Blacktop and sidewalks; flat*
SUITABLE FOR:	*All levels*
LOCATION:	*Honolulu (Map Region 1)*
COURSE:	🏃 🏃 🏃
PARKING:	🏃 🏃 🏃 🏃 🏃
AMENITIES:	🏃 🏃 🏃 🏃 🏃
SAFETY:	🏃 🏃 🏃 🏃
OVERALL RATING:	🏃 🏃 🏃 🏃

OVERVIEW Runners, joggers, and walkers of all levels enjoy this park for many reasons. Along with its easy access and ample parking, Kapi'olani Park has many rest rooms and water fountains. The route around the park is safe with no intersections to cross and is well-lit in the evenings. If you incorporate the zoo to increase the distance, you will need to cross Monsarrat Avenue twice, but Monsarrat is one-way through the park, which makes for a much safer crossing.

DIRECTIONS From downtown or beyond, take H1 east, and exit at King Street. Continue straight through the traffic light, and turn right on Kapahulu Avenue. Continue to the end of Kapahulu, turn left, and immediately bear to the left. Then make the first right into the free parking lot next to the Waikīkī Bandstand. From east Honolulu, take Kalaniana'ole Highway, and exit at Wai'alae Avenue. Take a left at the first traffic light, Kīlauea Avenue. After four traffic lights, take the next left on 'Elepaio Street. At the end of 'Elepaio, turn right on Kāhala Avenue. After you pass Fort Ruger Park (or Triangle Park), Kāhala Avenue becomes Diamond Head Road. Continue straight around the front of Diamond Head. At the stop sign, bear to the left down Kalākaua Avenue. At the end of the park, Kalākaua takes a sharp right and becomes Monsarrat Avenue. Make an immediate right into the bandstand parking area.

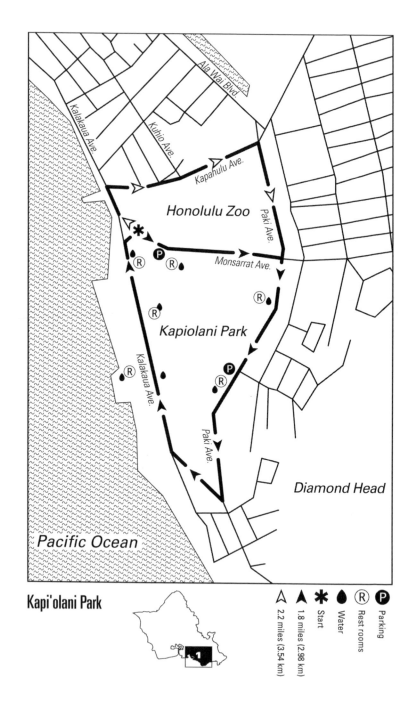

Honolulu Zoo

Kapiolani Park

Diamond Head

Pacific Ocean

Kalakaua Ave.

Kuhio Ave.

Ala Wai Blvd

Kapahulu Ave.

Paki Ave.

Monsarrat Ave.

Kalakaua Ave.

Paki Ave.

Kapi'olani Park

2.2 miles (3.54 km)

1.8 miles (2.98 km)

Start

Water

(R) Rest rooms

(P) Parking

COURSE Start at the Waikīkī Bandstand, an excellent meeting place with rest rooms, water fountains, and plenty of free parking. For the 1.85-mile loop, run along Monsarrat to the first traffic light at Pākī Avenue. Turn right on Pākī, and run along the designated running path. Pākī runs into Diamond Head Road at the south end of the park. Take a sharp right, and run along Kalākaua back to the bandstand. To increase the distance of the loop to 2.2 miles, simply add the Honolulu Zoo to your loop. As mentioned above, this will require crossing Monsarrat Avenue twice.

HIGHLIGHTS Kapiʻolani is the site for many local, national, and international events throughout the year. In the 1800s the park was the site of a horse-racing track but is best known today as the finish line for the Honolulu Marathon. Other events range from rugby, soccer, lacrosse, and softball, as well as numerous cultural fairs. Of course, Kapiʻolani Park is also the site of dozens of popular running races and triathlons. The number of runners in the park increases dramatically in the weeks leading up to the well-known events such as the Honolulu Marathon, which takes place the second Sunday in December, the Great Aloha Run on President's Day, and the Tinman Triathlon in mid-July.

CAUTIONS Check the events calendar before scheduling your training run at the park. Weekdays are usually not a problem, but weekends can get hectic. Concerts at the Waikīkī Shell, periodic parades, and special cultural events can make parking extremely difficult.

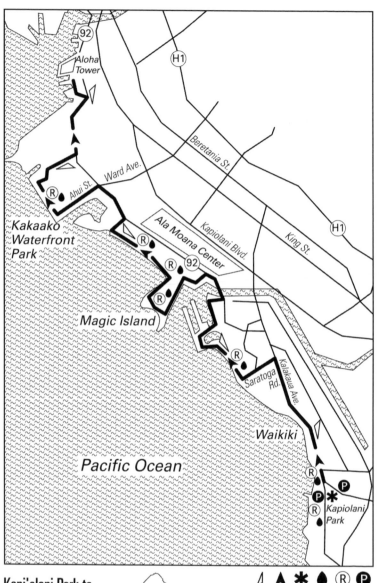

Aloha
Tower

92

H1

Ward Ave.

Beretania St.

H1

Ahui St.

*Kakaako
Waterfront
Park*

Ala Moana Center

R

R

Kapiolani Blvd.

King St.

92

R

Magic Island

R

Saratoga Rd.

Kalakaua Ave.

Waikiki

Pacific Ocean

R

R

*Kapiolani
Park*

Kapi'olani Park to
Aloha Tower

1

Return

Start

13.36 miles (21.5 km)

Water

R Rest rooms

P Parking

KAPI'OLANI PARK
TO ALOHA TOWER

DISTANCE:	*Short, medium, or long out-and-back course, up to 13.36 miles (21.5 km)*
SURFACE:	*Blacktop and cement sidewalks; a short stretch of sand; flat*
SUITABLE FOR:	*All levels*
LOCATION:	*Honolulu (Map Region 1)*
COURSE:	🏃 🏃 🏃
PARKING:	🏃 🏃 🏃 🏃
AMENITIES:	🏃 🏃 🏃 🏃
SAFETY:	🏃 🏃 🏃
OVERALL RATING:	🏃 🏃 🏃

OVERVIEW If you prefer the serenity of a nice, quiet nature trail run, this route may not appeal to you, but you shouldn't discount it either. Despite all the buildings and traffic, not too many city runs in the world can compare to this route for its spectacular ocean views. This course is designed to keep the runner as close to the water as possible throughout the entire run. Waikīkī gets pretty hot during the day, so this route is recommended for early mornings, late afternoons, or early evenings. If you time your run right, you will see a memorable sunset. This is a completely flat, out-and-back course; although the maximum out-and-back distance is 13.36 miles, you can easily transform it into a short or medium distance run.

DIRECTIONS The starting point for this run is Kapi'olani Park. To get to the park from windward or west O'ahu, take H1 east to the King Street exit. Continue to the second traffic light, and turn right on Kapahulu Avenue, which ends at Waikīkī Beach. At this point, take a left, and bear to the left at the "Y" in front of the Honolulu Zoo. A large, free parking lot will be on your right.

From east Honolulu, take H1 west to the Kapi'olani Boulevard exit. Once on Kapiʻolani Boulevard, move to the far left lane, and turn left on McCully. After crossing the Ala Wai Canal and Ala Wai Boulevard, turn left on Kalākaua Avenue, and continue through Waikīkī. In front of the Honolulu Zoo, stay to the left on Monsarrat, and take the first right into the free parking lot fronting the Waikīkī Bandstand at Kapiʻolani Park.

COURSE From the Kapiʻolani Park tennis courts, cross Kalākaua Avenue, and start your run along the beach walk just to the right of the Waikīkī Aquarium. Continue along the beach walk until you reach the Kūhiō Beach Pier adjacent to Kapahulu Avenue. At this point, pedestrian traffic gets fairly dense, and you will also be running against automobile traffic, so proceed with caution down the left-hand shoulder of Kalākaua Avenue. After about 1 mile, turn left on Saratoga Road. When Saratoga turns right into Kālia Road, continue straight across Kālia and down the beach access sidewalk. At the beach, turn right, and continue along the paved walkway. The sidewalk ends just after you pass the Hilton Hawaiian Village. At this point, continue across the sand around the left side of the Hilton Lagoon. After the lagoon, take a right on the road fronting the Ala Wai Boat Harbor. At the end of the harbor, the road makes a sharp right and brings you out to Ala Moana Boulevard. Take a left on Ala Moana, and proceed over the bridge crossing the Ala Wai Canal. After the bridge, take the first left into Ala Moana Beach Park. Staying on the left, follow the road into the park, then take the first left following the sidewalk along the water. Continue out around the perimeter of Magic Island, keeping the water on your left. The course will loop you around Magic Island and bring you back to Ala Moana Beach Park. Take a left, and continue along the beach walk.

At the end of Ala Moana Beach, the walkway will bring you back to Ala Moana Boulevard. Take another left, and continue along Ala Moana past the Kewalo Basin and Fisherman's Wharf. As soon as you pass Fisherman's Wharf, take another left on Ilalo Street, followed by another quick left on ʻĀhui Street. ʻĀhui will take you to the Kakaʻako Waterfront Park. At this point, you will be back on the beach walk. After you reach the end of the park, the walkway will turn to the right and wind its way back through the park. When you get to the first parking lot, cut through the lot, and take Ohe Street back to Ala Moana Boulevard. Turn left on Ala Moana, and continue down to the Aloha Tower Marketplace. Loop around the perimeter of the Aloha Tower pier, and return to Kapiʻolani Park, retracing your route.

HIGHLIGHTS You start and finish in the shadow of Diamond Head, run along Waikīkī Beach, and continue along the coastline of the most popular and recognizable tourist locations in the entire world. Just outside the Kakaʻako Waterfront Park is the future home for the University of Hawaiʻi's medical school and its extensive research facilities. As you approach the turnaround, you will pass a historic four-masted sailing ship, the *Falls of Clyde*, built in the 1870s in Scotland and used by the Matson Shipping Company to deliver goods to the Hawaiian Islands. Along with the *Falls of Clyde*, the Hawaiʻi Maritime Center offers a terrific display of Hawaiʻi's maritime history. The Aloha Tower was built in 1926 and served as a memorable landmark for cruise ships as they entered Honolulu Harbor. This ten-story tower was the tallest building in Honolulu for many years, dominating the Honolulu waterfront.

CAUTIONS This is a city run, so there is quite a bit of traffic. Through Waikīkī you will also encounter heavy pedestrian traffic. Both cars and pedestrians should be considered hazards through Waikīkī, because most of the people you encounter are so busy taking in the sights and sounds of Waikīkī, they will look right through you as you run along the road. Much of this run will be on sidewalks, so take it easy if you have foot or knee problems.

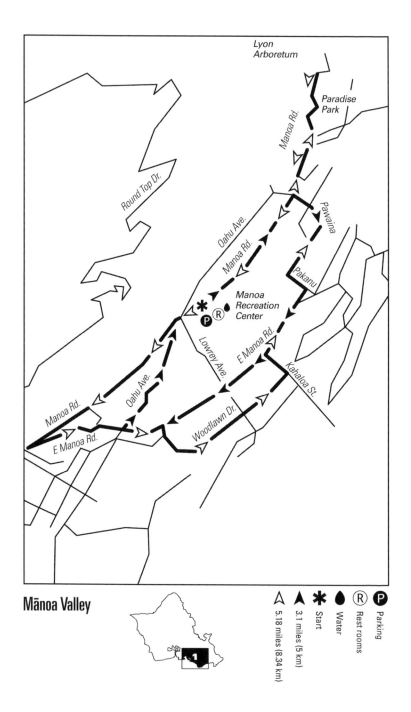

Lyon
Arboretum

Paradise
Park

Manoa Rd.

Round Top Dr.

Oahu Ave.

Manoa Rd.

Pawaina

Pakanu

Manoa
Recreation
Center

Lowrey Ave.

E Manoa Rd.

Kahaloa St.

Manoa Rd.

Oahu Ave.

E Manoa Rd.

Woodlawn Dr.

Mānoa Valley

1

5.18 miles (8.34 km)

3.1 miles (5 km)

Start

Water

Rest rooms

Parking

MĀNOA VALLEY

DISTANCE:	*3.1 or 5.18 miles (5 or 8.34 km)*
SURFACE:	*Blacktop; some grass shoulders; gentle hills*
SUITABLE FOR:	*All levels*
LOCATION:	*Honolulu (Map Region 1)*
COURSES:	🏃 🏃 🏃 🏃
PARKING:	🏃 🏃 🏃 🏃
AMENITIES:	🏃 🏃 🏃
SAFETY:	🏃 🏃 🏃
OVERALL RATING:	🏃 🏃 🏃 🏃

OVERVIEW Mānoa Valley offers a variety of running options. The roads heading to the back of the valley are all slightly uphill, and running out of the valley is mostly downhill. This old neighborhood has limited sidewalks, and some roads are narrow, but most offer grass shoulders. The Mānoa Recreation Center provides ample free public parking, along with public rest rooms and water. Mānoa is a beautiful, lush, green valley that gets its fair share of rain throughout the year.

DIRECTIONS From west and central Oʻahu, take H1 east to the Punahou Street exit. Stay in the left lane of the off-ramp. At the traffic light, turn left on Punahou Street. After the second traffic light, Punahou Street becomes Mānoa Road. At a "Y" intersection, stay to the left on Mānoa Road. At the first stop sign, continue straight through the five-way intersection continuing on Mānoa Road. Shortly after this intersection, you will come to the Mānoa Recreation Center on the right. Park in the recreation center's public parking area.

From east Oʻahu, follow H1 west, and take the University exit. The off-ramp will lead directly onto University Avenue. Continue up University Avenue past the University of Hawaiʻi. At the fifth traffic light, University Avenue becomes Oʻahu Avenue. Continue straight at this light, crossing East Mānoa Road. At the stop sign for the five-way intersection, take a gentle right on Mānoa Road, and continue for a short distance to the parking lot for the Mānoa Recreation Center.

COURSE For the 3.1-mile course, start on Mānoa Road fronting the Mānoa Recreation Center. Run toward the back of the valley. Turn right on Pāwaina Street, and follow Pāwaina down a slight hill as it doglegs to the right. Just before Pāwaina ends, turn left on Pakanu Street. Run up a slight rise, and take the first right on East Mānoa Road. Continue straight on East Mānoa Road past the Safeway and the fire station. Follow East Mānoa as it bends to the right up another small rise. At the top of the hill, turn right on Oʻahu Avenue. Follow Oʻahu Avenue until you reach a five-way intersection. At this point, take a slight bend to the right, and you will be back on Mānoa Road returning to the starting point at the recreation center.

The 5.18-mile course starts at the same point on Mānoa Road, but this time you head in the opposite direction toward the ocean (*makai*). Stay on Mānoa Road through the five-way intersection. Mānoa Road has no shoulder along this stretch, so stay on the left, and run along the grass shoulder. At the Mānoa Triangle, make a sharp left, heading back in the same direction you came but now on East Mānoa Road. Continue down East Mānoa Road straight through the traffic light at Oʻahu Avenue. At the second traffic light, turn right on Kolowalu. Kolowalu takes a dogleg bend to the left and becomes Woodlawn Drive. Continue on Woodlawn back into the valley. At the top of a small rise, turn left on Kahaloa. After one block, turn right back on East Mānoa Road. After 0.2 mile, East Mānoa splits. Stay to the left. After another block, make a left, and head down a short hill on Pakanu Street. At the bottom of the hill, turn right on Pāwaina Street. Follow Pāwaina Street as it curves to the left. At the top of a small rise, turn right on Mānoa Road. This stretch is an out-and-back section. Follow Mānoa Road to Paradise Park. At Paradise Park, turn around, and return back down Mānoa Road straight to the Mānoa Recreation Center.

HIGHLIGHTS Bordered by Tantalus Ridge on the left and Waʻahila Ridge on the right, Mānoa was primarily rich agricultural land and the site of a large dairy farm until the end of the nineteenth century. In the early twentieth century, a series of trolley tracks was built back into the valley, providing better accessibility and opening the valley up to development. The new housing development spread throughout lower Mānoa then slowly spread toward the back of the valley. Led by the descendants of the original missionaries, Mānoa became a favorite of the wealthy Honolulu business leaders. Many of the original homes from this early period can still be found throughout the valley. At the mouth of the valley is the University of Hawaiʻi's main campus. This research university first started as a land-grant college in 1907 and slowly grew into what is now an internationally renowned university with a diverse student population of 19,000. In the back of the valley is the Lyon Arboretum, an incredible outdoor laboratory of tropical plants from Hawaiʻi, the Pacific, and Asia. The arboretum is open to the public and provides well-manicured trails through 194 acres of unique plants and flowers. The arboretum boasts one of the largest collections of palms in the world. Next to the arboretum is a short trail that ascends 0.8 mile to the very back of the valley, ending at the base of Mānoa Falls. In the opposite direction, about midway to the mouth of the valley along Mānoa Road is the Waiʻoli Tea House. This historic site was built during the early development of Mānoa and is wonderful for a casual lunch or a formal high tea. At the base of the valley to the west of the university is Punahou School, founded in 1841, which is the largest independent school in the country and the oldest private school west of the Mississippi.

CAUTIONS Mānoa Valley receives a large amount of precipitation, so prepare to get wet. More often than not, however, the rain comes in a pleasant and refreshing mist. Streetlights are limited on all but the main thoroughfares, so if you plan to run after dark, choose a route that offers better lighting and wider shoulders. A number of the main roads are quite narrow, and runners must stay on the grass shoulders. These shoulders can be uneven with outcroppings of tree roots, so watch your footing.

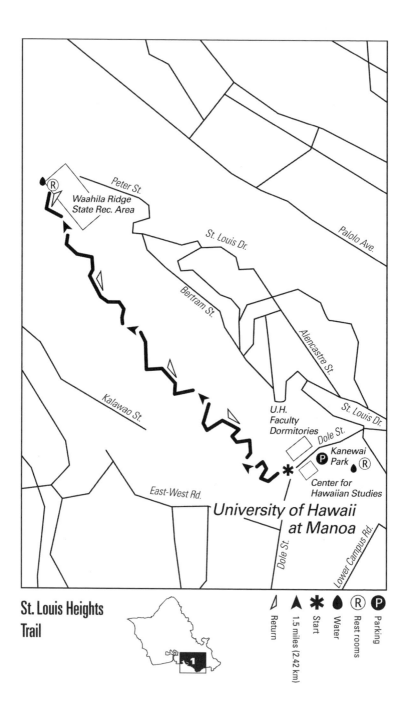

Peter St.

Waahila Ridge
State Rec. Area

St. Louis Dr.

Palolo Ave.

Bertram St.

Alencastre St.

St. Louis Dr.

Kalawao St.

U.H.
Faculty
Dormitories

Dole St.

Kanewai
Park

P

R

Center for
Hawaiian Studies

East-West Rd.

University of Hawaii
at Manoa

Dole St.

Lower Campus Rd.

St. Louis Heights
Trail

Return

1.5 miles (2.42 km)

Start

Water

R Rest rooms

P Parking

ST. LOUIS HEIGHTS TRAIL

DISTANCE:	*1.5 miles (2.42 km)*
SURFACE:	*Trail; very rugged and steep*
SUITABLE FOR:	*Advanced; speed training*
LOCATION:	*Honolulu (Map Region 1)*
COURSE:	👟 👟
PARKING:	👟 👟
AMENITIES:	👟 👟
SAFETY:	👟
OVERALL RATING:	👟 👟

OVERVIEW An extremely challenging, 800-foot hill climb on a dirt and rock trail, this course has become dangerous due to the increased number of downhill mountain bikers using this trail. As more and more trails have been closed to these brave souls, the St. Louis Heights trail has seen a marked increase in these downhill aficionados.

This trail is steep with many blind turns; use extreme caution if you choose to run this course. The downhill bikers are moving very fast, and they don't expect to see runners coming up the other way. Check with the local bike tour companies to see when the bikers will be using the trail. Always remember that the bikers have the right-of-way on this course, so run defensively.

DIRECTIONS The trailhead is located on Dole Street between East-West Road and the University of Hawai'i's faculty dormitory complex. From downtown and west O'ahu, take H1 east, and take the King Street exit. After exiting, merge to the far left lane, and take a left at the first traffic light. Drive under the H1, take a left on St. Louis Drive at the second traffic light, and stay in the left lane. Just as St. Louis starts heading uphill, take a left on Dole Street. Continue through a traffic light and past Kānewai Park on your left. Parking is very limited in this area, but try to park at the Kānewai

Park or along the street. The trailhead is a short walk along Dole from the Kānewai Park.

From east Honolulu and Hawai'i Kai, take H1 west to the University Avenue exit. On University Avenue, take the first right on Dole Street. The trailhead is on the left a short distance after the second traffic light.

COURSE The trailhead is on Dole Street, approximately 20 meters west of the University of Hawai'i faculty dormitory complex and across the street from the Center for Hawaiian Studies. The trail starts with a steep ascent with many sharp switchbacks through dry, thorny brush and loose rocks. After 0.25 mile, the trail straightens out slightly and begins to follow the ridgeline, offering some terrific views of Mānoa Valley. As you continue along the ridgeline, the trail widens as it gains elevation, eventually running through a beautiful stand of pine trees before opening up into the Wa'ahila State Park. This climb is very short, but challenging, and it does not end there since you still need to get back down. On the descent, after the trail narrows, you will come to a fork in the trail marked by a telephone pole. Go straight at the fork. Although this route has a number of difficult sections, it is much gentler than the trail that splits off to the right.

HIGHLIGHTS This trail provides a tough hill climb, along with an excellent look at Mānoa Valley. Due to the shortness of the trail, it will give you a good, hard workout that you can finish in a relatively short time. From the Wa'ahila State Park, the Wa'ahila Ridge Trail continues from the back of the park and runs along the ridge for another 2.4 miles. Although this section of the trail is not conducive to running, it lets you see both Mānoa and Pālolo Valleys, and it makes for a great hike to cool down from your run.

CAUTIONS Run this trail with extreme caution and only after checking with the local mountain bike tour companies. Even then, you should be very cautious when approaching blind turns. This trail is quite dangerous and is not recommended for anyone without many years of experience.

TANTALUS LOOP

DISTANCE:	*10 miles (16.1 km)*
SURFACE:	*Blacktop; very hilly*
SUITABLE FOR:	*Intermediate to advanced*
LOCATION:	*Honolulu (Map Region 1)*
COURSE:	彑 彑 彑
PARKING:	彑 彑
AMENITIES:	彑 彑
SAFETY:	彑 彑
OVERALL RATING:	彑 彑 彑

OVERVIEW The Tantalus Loop is a hill run, period, and is not for the casual jogger. This winding route climbs for 5 miles to just over 2,000 feet, followed by 5 miles of winding descent. Do not attempt this run unless you are prepared for 2 hours of strenuous exercise. On the other hand, the Tantalus Loop offers a break from the heat of Honolulu, along with beautiful stretches of tropical rain forest and large stands of bamboo. The loop also includes unparalleled views of downtown Honolulu, Waikīkī, and Mānoa Valley.

DIRECTIONS From east Honolulu, take H1 west, to the Wilder Avenue exit. Follow Wilder, and turn right on Makiki Street. On Makiki Street, cross three intersections, and take a left on Makiki Heights Drive. Park along Makiki Heights Drive across from Archie Baker Park. From west Honolulu, exit off H1 east at Punahou Street. Stay in the left lane, and turn left on Punahou Street. At the second traffic light, turn left on Wilder Avenue, and follow the directions listed above.

COURSE From Archie Baker Park, run up along Makiki Heights Drive. At a "T" intersection, turn right on Tantalus Drive. Follow Tantalus Drive to the summit where it becomes Round Top Drive. Round Top Drive will take you on a 5-mile descent back to Archie

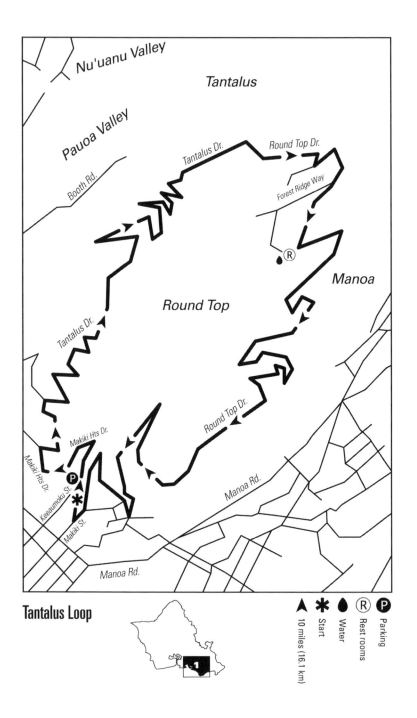

Nu'uanu Valley

Tantalus

Pauoa Valley

Booth Rd.

Tantalus Dr.

Round Top Dr.

Forest Ridge Way

Ⓡ

Manoa

Tantalus Dr.

Round Top

Makiki Hts Dr.

Round Top Dr.

Makiki Hts Dr.

Ⓟ

Keeaumoku St.

Makiki St.

Manoa Rd.

Manoa Rd.

Tantalus Loop

1

▲ 10 miles (16.1 km)

✱ Start

💧 Water

Ⓡ Rest rooms

Ⓟ Parking

Baker Park. On the descent, take a short detour at Puʻuʻualakaʻa Park for a spectacular scenic view, not to mention the only public rest rooms along the loop.

HIGHLIGHTS Cool temperatures, beautiful tropical foliage, and spectacular scenic views abound along this challenging loop. Tantalus is also well known for its abundance of running trails that crisscross this ridge, and this trail system, further described in the next course, is the location for one of the country's toughest-rated 100-mile ultra-marathons, the HURT Trail 100, sponsored by the Hawaiʻi Ultra Running Team.

CAUTIONS This narrow, winding road has many blind turns. Traffic is relatively light, but you need to assume that the drivers you do encounter are not expecting to see runners along this stretch, so you must be prepared to take evasive action. Tantalus also gets quite a bit of rain, so watch for slippery moss-covered stretches of road on both sides of the summit. Finally, except for a small park around the 7-mile mark, there are no water stations, so be sure to bring your own supply.

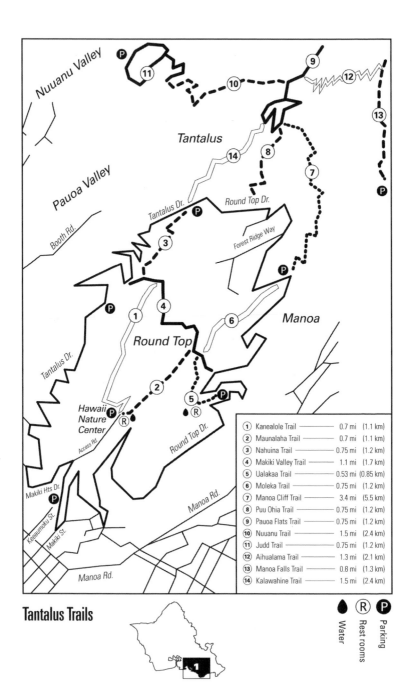

Tantalus Trails

① Kanealole Trail	0.7 mi	(1.1 km)
② Maunalaha Trail	0.7 mi	(1.1 km)
③ Nahuina Trail	0.75 mi	(1.2 km)
④ Makiki Valley Trail	1.1 mi	(1.7 km)
⑤ Ualakaa Trail	0.53 mi	(0.85 km)
⑥ Moleka Trail	0.75 mi	(1.2 km)
⑦ Manoa Cliff Trail	3.4 mi	(5.5 km)
⑧ Puu Ohia Trail	0.75 mi	(1.2 km)
⑨ Pauoa Flats Trail	0.75 mi	(1.2 km)
⑩ Nuuanu Trail	1.5 mi	(2.4 km)
⑪ Judd Trail	0.75 mi	(1.2 km)
⑫ Aihualama Trail	1.3 mi	(2.1 km)
⑬ Manoa Falls Trail	0.8 mi	(1.3 km)
⑭ Kalawahine Trail	1.5 mi	(2.4 km)

Water   Ⓡ Rest rooms   Ⓟ Parking

TANTALUS TRAILS

DISTANCE:	*Varies*
SURFACE:	*Trails; very hilly*
SUITABLE FOR:	*Experienced trail runners*
LOCATION:	*Honolulu (Map Region 1)*
COURSE:	🏃 🏃 🏃
PARKING:	🏃 🏃
AMENITIES:	🏃 🏃
SAFETY:	🏃 🏃
OVERALL RATING:	🏃 🏃 🏃

OVERVIEW The Tantalus trails are a series of short trails that criss-cross Tantalus from Makiki to Nuʻuanu. Each of the individual trails connects to various other trails. By combining multiple trails, you can run these trails for days without covering the same course twice. The Tantalus trail system is very hilly and often wet and slippery. These trails are the favorites of Oʻahu's hardcore trail runners, but they can seem daunting and challenging to the novice trail runner.

DIRECTIONS From east Honolulu, take H1 west, to the Wilder Avenue exit. Follow Wilder, and turn right on Makiki Street. On Makiki Street cross three intersections, and take a left on Makiki Heights Drive. Follow Makiki Heights Drive for about 0.5 mile to the first horseshoe turn. At the horseshoe, take a right off Makiki Heights Drive, and follow the signs to the Hawaiʻi Nature Center, the most popular starting point for a series of trails. From west Honolulu, exit off H1 east at Punahou Street. Stay in the left lane, and turn left on Punahou Street. At the second traffic light, turn left on Wilder Avenue, and follow the directions listed above.

COURSE The Tantalus Trails are actually a spiderweb series of 14 different trails that crisscross their way across Tantalus and into the bordering valleys of Mānoa, Pauoa, and Nuʻuanu. You can create any number of courses by mixing and matching the various trails, but I will focus on only two, one long and one midrange. All numbers following trail names refer to the Tantalus Trails map.

The long course starts at the Hawai'i Nature Center. From this starting point, you can choose to start on the Maunalaha Trail (2), which will take you to the right on a steep climb of the east ridge of Makiki Valley, or you can start to the left on the Kanealole Trail (1). My recommendation is to start on the Kanealole Trail and take the loop clockwise. The Kanealole Trail offers a gentler climb at the start, which allows for some warm-up before you hit the steeper ascents. This trail follows the Kanealole Stream as it winds its way back into the Makiki Valley. After 0.7 mile, the trail connects with the Makiki Valley Trail (4). Turn left on the Makiki Valley Trail. After a short stretch that includes three steep switchbacks, you will come to the junction with Nahuina Trail (3). Take a right on the Nahuina Trail, and continue to climb along the west side of the Makiki Valley Ridge. After four switchbacks, the Nahuina Trail ends at Tantalus Drive. Turn right on Tantalus Drive, and follow the pavement as it narrows to a one-lane road. As soon as the road widens, look for the next trailhead on the left. The Kalawahine Trail (14) takes you along the ridge bordering Pauoa Valley. As you wind in and out of several gulches, you will be rewarded with terrific views of the valley far below. After 1.5 miles, this trail ends at the Pauoa Flats Trail (9). Continue straight on the Pauoa Flats Trail. As you continue along the Pauoa Flats, the trail is covered with a challenging series of exposed roots and rocks, so take this section slowly. If the trail is wet, these roots become extremely slippery. On your left, the Nu'uanu Trail (10) comes up, heads down into the Nu'uanu Valley, and hooks up with the Judd Trail (11).

Continue straight past this junction. You will come upon the junction for the Aihualama Trail (12), which is on your right in the midst of a stand of bamboo. This trail follows a very steep and winding path deep into the back of Mānoa Valley. Again, continue straight past this junction until you reach the Nu'uanu Valley overlook. At this point, the trail is closed, so, after enjoying the spectacular view, turn around, and retrace your steps to the Mānoa Cliff Trail (7). Take a left on the Mānoa Cliff Trail. This trail takes you around the Tantalus Crater and then out along the cliffs that contour along the ridgeline high above Mānoa Valley.

Watch for erosion along stretches of this trail. The Mānoa Cliff Trail ends when it runs into the upper reaches of Round Top Drive. You will pick up the Moleka Trail (6) directly across the road. The Moleka Trail follows along the upper edge of Makiki Valley, traversing high above the Moleka Stream. After 0.75 mile, the Moleka Trail ends at the junction with the Makiki Valley Trail (4). Turn right on the Makiki Valley Trail for a very short stretch before making a left on the Maunalaha Trail (2). This trail follows a steep route down the ridgeline, descending to the valley floor and ending back at the Hawai'i Nature Center.

The midrange trail begins after a 3-mile drive up Round Top Drive. Enter the Pu'u'ualaka'a State Park. The park is open from 7:00 AM to 7:45 PM from April 1 to Labor Day and from 7:00 AM to 6:45 PM from Labor Day until March 31. Just inside the entrance on the right-hand side is the trailhead for the 'Ualaka'a Trail (5). Take the 'Ualaka'a Trail through a densely forested area. After a short climb, the trail comes to a four-way intersection with the Maunalaha (2), Makiki Valley (4), and Moleka Trails (6). Take the Moleka Trail, and continue to climb through heavy stands of bamboo. As the trail comes out onto Round Top Drive, continue straight across the road, and catch the trailhead for the Mānoa Cliff Trail (7). Follow the Mānoa Cliff Trail until it meets the Pauoa Flats Trail (9) and soon junctions with the Kalawahine (14). Continue in a counterclockwise direction around along the ridge bordering the Pauoa Valley.

As the Kalawahine Trail ends, continue along Tantalus Drive for less than 0.1 mile. At the end of the guardrail on the left is the start of the Nahuina Trail (3). Follow this trail down into Makiki Valley along four steep switchbacks. When you get to the junction with the Makiki Valley Trail (4), take a left, and cut across the upper reaches of the valley until you reach the junction with the 'Ualaka'a Trail (5). Follow the 'Ualaka'a Trail back to the Pu'u'ualaka'a State Park. After retrieving your car, drive back into the park to find public rest rooms and drinking water. This park also offers a terrific view that stretches from Koko Head to the 'Ewa plains.

HIGHLIGHTS The Tantalus trails not only offer some of the most stunning views on O'ahu, but they also provide the experienced trail runner with difficult climbs and technical descents. This system of trails makes up what has become one of the most challenging 100-mile ultra–trail races in the country, the HURT Trail 100. This extreme event, with over 23,000 feet of ascents and descents, was first held in 2001 and has been held during the third weekend in January ever since. Other trail runs are held here throughout the year and are sponsored by both the Hawai'i Ultra Running Team (HURT) and the Mid-Pacific Road Runners.

CAUTIONS As described earlier, this elevated region gets plenty of rainfall throughout the year, so these trails tend to stay wet. Erosion along the trails has exposed many tree roots that run at odd angles across the trails, making for slippery footing. Finally, due to the nature of this trail system, you can easily get lost, so you should hook up with someone familiar with these trails until you know your way around. A great place to locate runners experienced with the Tantalus Trail system is by contacting the Mid-Pacific Road Runners at *www.mprrc.com*, or by calling them at (808) 295-6777.

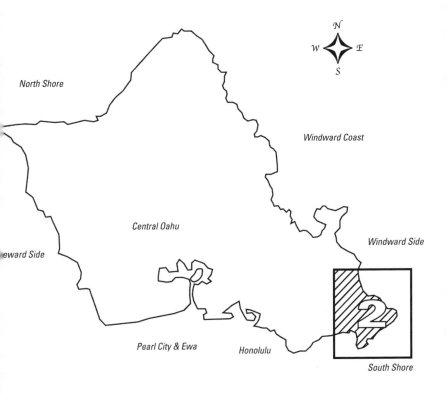

North Shore

Windward Coast

Central Oahu

Windward Side

eward Side

Pearl City & Ewa

Honolulu

South Shore

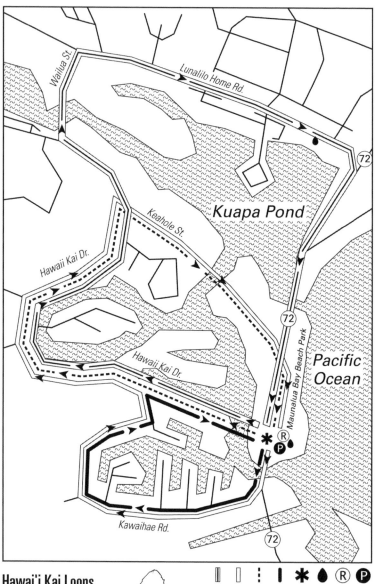

Kuapa Pond

72

Wailua St.

Lunalilo Home Rd.

Keahole St.

Hawaii Kai Dr.

72

Hawaii Kai Dr.

Maunalua Bay Beach Park

Pacific Ocean

Kawaihae Rd.

72

Hawai'i Kai Loops

▯ 4.71 miles (7.58 km)	▯ 4 miles (6.44 km)	⋮ 2.37 miles (3.81 km)
❙ 1.4 miles (2.25 km)	✱ Start	◗ Water
Ⓡ Rest rooms	Ⓟ Parking	

HAWAI'I KAI LOOPS

DISTANCE:	*1.4, 2.37, 4, or 4.71 miles*
	(2.25, 3.81, 6.44, or 7.58 km)
SURFACE:	*Blacktop; some sidewalks; flat*
SUITABLE FOR:	*All levels*
LOCATION:	*South Shore (Map Region 2)*
COURSE:	🏃 🏃 🏃 🏃
PARKING:	🏃 🏃 🏃 🏃
AMENITIES:	🏃 🏃 🏃
SAFETY:	🏃 🏃 🏃 🏃
OVERALL RATING:	🏃 🏃 🏃 🏃

OVERVIEW These four flat courses run through the residential neighborhood of Hawai'i Kai and are of varying distances. You can choose to run one loop or a combination of loops that will provide you with short- to medium-distance runs without having to duplicate your loops. Even though you will see many runners and bikers, the roads and sidewalks are wide, and there are few major intersections. Hawai'i Kai is a dry and hot area, but the frequent cooling trade winds make even afternoon runs bearable. This well-lit area is also conducive to safe nighttime running. The starting point for all four loops is the parking lot of Maunalua Bay Beach Park, which offers rest rooms and a water fountain.

DIRECTIONS From west and central O'ahu, take H1 east to the end. The H1 ends at exit 27 in Kāhala and becomes Kalaniana'ole Highway (72). Continue 5 miles along Kalaniana'ole until you come to Hawai'i Kai Drive. Across from Hawai'i Kai Drive is the entrance to Maunalua Bay Beach Park. Turn right into the beach park parking area, which provides a good starting point for all four of the loops. From the windward side of O'ahu, you can take either Likelike Highway (63) or the Pali Highway (61) to Honolulu. Then follow H1 to Hawai'i Kai. If you live on the Kailua or Waimānalo side, you may find it much easier and a lot more picturesque to follow Kalaniana'ole Highway around the south shore to Hawai'i Kai.

COURSE For the short 1.4-mile loop, start from the beach park, and walk across to the mountain (*mauka*) side of the highway. Turn left, and run Honolulu-bound along Kalaniana'ole Highway. Turn right on Kawaihae, and follow this looping road around to Hawai'i Kai Drive. A right on Hawai'i Kai Drive will take you right back to your starting point.

The 2.37-mile loop follows Hawai'i Kai Drive toward the mountains. Follow the road as it curves to the right and takes you past Hawai'i Kai Recreation Center and the O'ahu Tennis Club. When you get to Keāhole, turn right back to Kalaniana'ole Highway.

The 4-mile loop starts off following the course of the first loop, but at Hawai'i Kai Drive, turn left instead of right. Then follow the directions for the second loop.

Finally, the 4.71-mile loop follows the second loop until you get to Keāhole. This time take a left, and continue following Hawai'i Kai Drive to the first traffic light. Turn right on Wailua, and run up over the Kuapā Pond Bridge. Wailua ends at Lunalilo Home Road. At this point, turn right, and head back to Kalaniana'ole Highway. When you get back to the highway, turn right, and you will be on your way back to the Maunalua Bay Beach Park. Since all four loops connect, it becomes easy to mix and match the different loops to reach the distance you want.

HIGHLIGHTS Hawai'i Kai is a middle- to upper-middle-class suburb of Honolulu that was the brainchild of Henry J. Kaiser. Kaiser made a name for himself as a great industrialist during the first half of the twentieth century. During World War II, Kaiser was one of the nation's largest shipbuilders. Innovations introduced by Kaiser revolutionized the shipbuilding industry. Following the war, Kaiser expanded from steel and aluminum manufacturing into home building and health care, pioneering today's HMOs with the development of health care at a set fee. Kaiser also developed the Hilton Hawaiian Village in Waikīkī. Hawai'i Kai had been a vast marshland known as Kuapā Pond before Kaiser had the area dredged and reformed to create this housing development interspersed with waterways.

CAUTIONS The most dangerous part of this course is crossing Kalaniana'ole Highway. Fortunately, this only has to be done at the start and finish, so it does not interfere with your run. This course is popular with cyclists, so you should either stay on the sidewalks or run facing traffic so you can see the bikes coming.

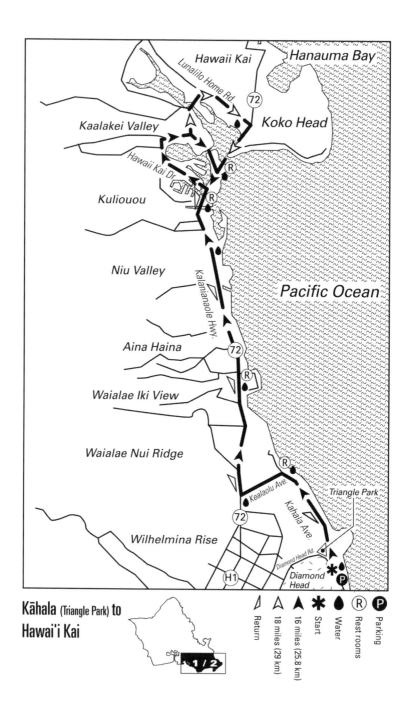

Hanauma Bay

Hawaii Kai

Lunalilo Home Rd.

72

Koko Head

Kaalakei Valley

Hawaii Kai Dr.

R

Kuliouou

R

Niu Valley

Kalanianaole Hwy.

Pacific Ocean

72

Aina Haina

R

Waialae Iki View

Waialae Nui Ridge

R

Triangle Park

Kealaolu Ave.

Kahala Ave.

72

Wilhelmina Rise

Diamond Head Rd.

H1

Diamond Head

P

Kāhala (Triangle Park) to
Hawai'i Kai

1/2

Return

18 miles (29 km)

16 miles (25.8 km)

Start

Water

R Rest rooms

P Parking

KĀHALA (TRIANGLE PARK) TO HAWAI'I KAI

DISTANCE:	*Short, medium, or long out-and-back course, up to 18 miles (29 km)*
SURFACE:	*Blacktop and sidewalks; flat*
SUITABLE FOR:	*All levels*
LOCATION:	*South Shore and Honolulu (Map Regions 1 and 2)*
COURSE:	🏃 🏃 🏃
PARKING:	🏃 🏃
AMENITIES:	🏃 🏃 🏃
SAFETY:	🏃 🏃 🏃 🏃
OVERALL RATING:	🏃 🏃 🏃

OVERVIEW This excellent out-and-back course is perfectly suited for those long, slow training runs because the entire route is flat with very few major intersections. The distance varies depending on how far you want to run. You can easily add additional miles by starting at Kapi'olani Park instead of Triangle Park. The downside of this route is that the long stretch along Kalaniana'ole Highway is not very attractive. The highway has a wide bike lane and sidewalk, but it also has a steady flow of commuter traffic. Triangle Park is a popular starting point, but it lacks amenities. The park has a water fountain, but no rest room facilities.

DIRECTIONS From downtown and west O'ahu, take H1 east, exiting at Wai'alae Avenue. Continue on Wai'alae, and turn right at the second traffic light onto Hunakai. Follow Hunakai until it ends at Kāhala Avenue. Turn right on Kāhala, and continue to the base of Diamond Head. Triangle Park is located on the right just before Kāhala Avenue becomes Diamond Head Road. Street parking is available along the southeast side of the park and in the surrounding neighborhood. Triangle Park is a meeting place for bicyclists, so parking can be limited on weekend mornings.

From the south shore of Oʻahu, take Kalanianaʻole Highway (72) toward Honolulu. Exit at Waiʻalae Avenue, and take the first left on Kīlauea Avenue. Follow Kīlauea for just less than 1 mile, turning left on Hunakai. Once on Hunakai, follow the directions described above.

COURSE From Triangle Park, head down Kāhala Avenue. At the stop sign, turn left on Kealaʻolu Avenue. Kealaʻolu borders the famous Waiʻalae Country Club on your right. At the end of Kealaʻolu, turn right, and head up the on-ramp to Kalanianaʻole Highway. Simply follow the highway for as long as you want to go. Once you have reached your limit, turn around, and head back the same route you came. If you are ready for the full course, continue along the highway until you enter Hawaiʻi Kai. Take a left on Hawaiʻi Kai Drive, and continue along this road as it winds its way through this beautiful residential community. If you are not ready for the full distance, turn right on Keāhole Drive, and within 0.5 mile you will be back to Kalanianaʻole and heading home. For the full run, when you hit Keāhole, turn left, and then take a right on Wailua Street. Wailua ends at Lunalilo Home Road. From here, turn right, and you will be heading back to Kalanianaʻole Highway.

HIGHLIGHTS This route follows the Honolulu Marathon course, and the marathon mile marks are painted on the right-hand shoulder of the road. This feature is nice if you are interested in keeping track of your mile splits. Plus, most weekends you will find that you are running along with many of Honolulu's running and biking enthusiasts.

This route connects two of Oʻahu's most exclusive neighborhoods, Kāhala and Portlock, and will take you past the incredible gated community of Hawaiʻi Loa Ridge. If multimillion-dollar homes appeal to you, you will have plenty to get excited about along this route. At the far end of Kāhala, the course turns left and runs along the edge of the Waiʻalae Country Club, site of the PGA Tour's Sony Open, once known as the Hawaiian Open.

CAUTIONS This route is long and gets hot during the day, so you should schedule your runs for early mornings or evenings, when a steady trade wind breeze is usually present to keep you cool. Also, be sure to hydrate yourself throughout your run. A number of small public beach parks are along Kalaniana'ole, and they all have water fountains and rest rooms. In addition to the parks, a number of other water stations are along the course; study the course map, locate these stations, and drink, drink, drink. If you plan to run during the evenings, be sure to wear reflective gear. You will notice many fast-moving cars, and some stretches are not well lit. Bikers also use this route to train, so avoid blocking the bike lane. Either stay far to the right or on the sidewalk. There are not many places for bikers to train on O'ahu, so be courteous and share the road. Finally, the majority of Kalaniana'ole Highway is cement, so this route can be hard on your legs. If you have foot or knee problems, you may want to limit your time on this course.

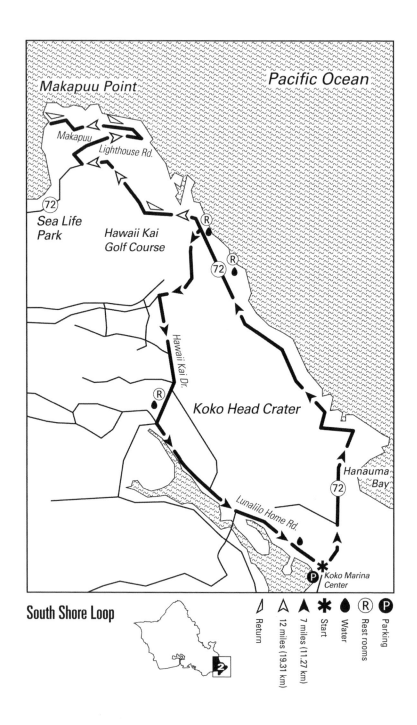

Pacific Ocean

Makapuu Point

Makapuu

Lighthouse Rd.

72

Sea Life
Park

Hawaii Kai
Golf Course

Ⓡ

72

Ⓡ

Hawaii Kai Dr.

Ⓡ

Koko Head Crater

Hanauma
Bay

72

Lunalilo Home Rd.

Ⓟ Koko Marina
Center

South Shore Loop

Return	12 miles (19.31 km)	7 miles (11.27 km)	Start	Water	Rest rooms	Parking

SOUTH SHORE LOOP

DISTANCE:	*7 or 12 miles (11.27 or 19.31 km)*
SURFACE:	*Blacktop; rolling hills*
SUITABLE FOR:	*Intermediate to advanced*
LOCATION:	*South Shore (Map Region 2)*
COURSE:	🏃 🏃 🏃 🏃
PARKING:	🏃 🏃 🏃 🏃
AMENITIES:	🏃 🏃 🏃
SAFETY:	🏃 🏃 🏃
OVERALL RATING:	🏃 🏃 🏃 🏃

OVERVIEW This course has it all—challenging hills, spectacular views, and very few intersections, so you can maintain a comfortable running rhythm. An excellent course for a long weekend run that boasts a beautiful stretch of coastline, this route is recommended for the early morning or early evening when it is not as hot, and traffic tends to be lighter.

DIRECTIONS Take H1 east toward Hawai'i Kai. H1 becomes Kalaniana'ole Highway (72) after passing through Kāhala. Continue on Kalaniana'ole Highway for approximately 4.5 miles. Park at the Koko Marina Shopping Center on the corner of Kalaniana'ole Highway and Lunalilo Home Road.

COURSE Start at the Koko Marina Shopping Center, and head east up along the Kalaniana'ole Highway. A long uphill will provide an excellent warm-up and bring you to the entrance of Hanauma Bay. Continue past the Hanauma Bay entrance, and stay on the right side of the highway. In this tremendously beautiful section, if you are lucky, you will spot some whales frolicking off the coast (only during the spring months).

After you pass the blowhole parking area, a short downhill section begins before the road flattens out for a long stretch along Sandy Beach. If you are in need of water or a rest room, detour through the beach park, where you will find two separate rest room facilities with water fountains; otherwise, continue straight on Kalanianaʻole Highway. At the traffic light, the 7-mile course turns left on Kealahou Road and heads back to Hawaiʻi Kai, but for the 12-mile course continue along the highway. Cactus flourish in this dry area, and the temperatures can get pretty hot, but fairly strong trade winds will keep you relatively cool.

About 0.5 mile past the entrance to the Hawaiʻi Kai Championship Golf Club, turn off the highway at the Military Access Road to the Makapuʻu Lighthouse. The 1-mile access road is closed to vehicular traffic and takes you on a 640-foot climb to the Makapuʻu Lighthouse lookout. This is a natural place to take a short break before heading back. Check out the view of the windward coast, and see if you can spot any whales.

On the return, run back the same way that you came. Please note that the cooling trade winds are now at your back and are not quite as refreshing as they were on the way out. When you get to the first traffic light at Kealahou Road, turn right. Follow this road as it winds through Queen's Gate community development. Turn left at Hawaiʻi Kai Drive. After a short climb, the road bears to the right and heads down into Hawaiʻi Kai. Close to the bottom of the hill, rest rooms and a water fountain are next to the soccer field. Turn left on Lunalilo Home Road, and it's a straight, flat 2 miles to complete the route at the Koko Marina Shopping Center.

HIGHLIGHTS As you begin this run, you will be facing the 1,208-foot-high Koko Head Crater. The Hawaiian name for Koko Head Crater is "Kohelepelepe" which, when translated, means "fringed vagina." You may need to pick up a book on Hawaiian folklore to get the story behind that name, but Koko Head Crater offers a challenging hike straight up its side, where an old tram ride used to be located. Hanauma Bay, a marine sanctuary in a crater of an extinct volcano, is next on your run. Although the course does not include this spot, you can certainly make a quick detour to check out this state underwater park. Take the entry road down to the parking area. To the right of the visitor's center, a viewpoint provides an outstanding panorama of this spectacular bay. Hanauma Bay has been forced to place some restrictions on the number of visitors in an attempt to protect its reef's fragile ecosystem, but it still seems to be crowded most of the time. If you decide to take a dip, please be sure to stay off the reef, and avoid feeding the fish.

Continuing along the rugged coastline, you will spot Hālona Cove, a beautiful little spit of sand nestled in between the lava cliffs. This beach was made famous in the classic film *From Here to Eternity*. Next to this cove is the Hālona Blowhole. When the waves and currents are right, this lava tube creates some amazing water plumes. Below the blowhole lookout, Sandy Beach spreads out along the flattened coast. Do not let the beauty of this beach fool you; more necks are broken in this beach's shore break than on all other Hawai'i beaches combined, so unless you are an experienced bodysurfer, leave your ego at home, and just enjoy the view.

From the top of the Makapu'u Lighthouse lookout, the view of the windward coast includes Makapu'u Beach, with probably the most popular bodysurfing in Hawai'i, and Rabbit Island. After the long run to the top of this lookout, as you squint through the sweat in your eyes, you may think this island looks like a rabbit, but it was actually named for its use as a site for harvesting rabbits in the late 1800s. The final stretch of this run will take you along Lunalilo Home Road, named for the home established for elderly Hawaiians by the will of King Lunalilo.

CAUTIONS After the first hill, the shoulder becomes quite narrow for about 2 miles, so use extreme caution. If you plan to run during the evening or early morning, wear a reflective vest. This portion of Kalaniana'ole Highway gets many large tour buses during the day, but, as long as you run single file and stay close to the guardrail, this run is relatively safe and a real beauty. This stretch is also a well-known training site for bikers, and there is not enough room for bikers and runners to coexist. Since they are riding with traffic and the shoulders are narrow, this is one stretch where running with the flow of traffic on the right-hand shoulder is recommended.

REGION 3

WINDWARD SIDE

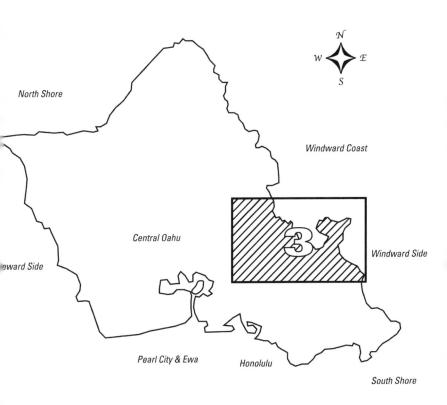

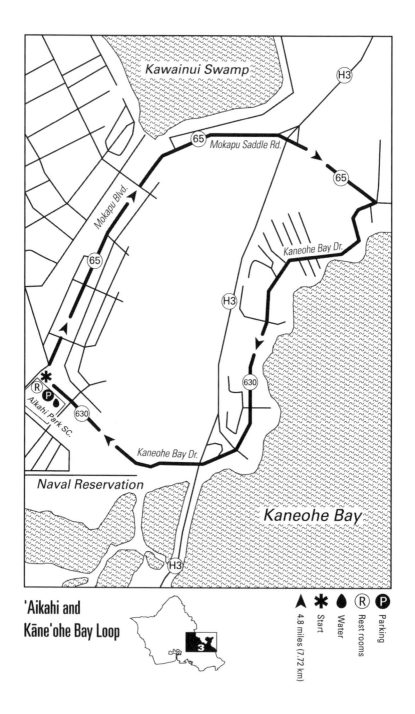

Kawainui Swamp

H3

65 Mokapu Saddle Rd.

65

Mokapu Blvd.

Kaneohe Bay Dr.

65

H3

630

R P
Aikahi Park SC.

630

Kaneohe Bay Dr.

Naval Reservation

Kaneohe Bay

H3

'Aikahi and
Kāne'ohe Bay Loop

3

4.8 miles (7.72 km)   Start   Water   R Rest rooms   P Parking

'AIKAHI AND KĀNE'OHE BAY LOOP

DISTANCE:	*4.8 miles (7.72 km)*
SURFACE:	*Blacktop and sidewalks; hilly*
SUITABLE FOR:	*All levels*
LOCATION:	*Windward Side (Map Region 3)*
COURSE:	🏃 🏃 🏃
PARKING:	🏃 🏃 🏃 🏃
AMENITIES:	🏃 🏃
SAFETY:	🏃 🏃 🏃
OVERALL RATING:	🏃 🏃 🏃

OVERVIEW This convenient 4.8-mile loop features a long hill, along with a number of small, rolling hills. Few shaded areas are along this course, so you should not run the course at midday. Early morning or late afternoons are the best times to run this course. Plenty of parking is usually available at the 'Aikahi Park Shopping Center, and, although there are no public rest rooms or water fountains along the course, the Safeway at the shopping center has rest rooms, plenty of water, and sports drinks for purchase.

DIRECTIONS From east Honolulu, take the Pali Highway (61) exit off H1. Follow the Pali Highway to Kailua. After passing through the Pali Tunnels, take a left at the first traffic light (Kamehameha Highway). From Kamehameha Highway, take the H3 exit to Kailua. Follow H3 to the very end, taking the last exit before the highway runs into the Kāne'ohe Marine Base. At the end of the off-ramp, turn left on Kāne'ohe Bay Drive. After one traffic signal, turn left into the 'Aikahi Park Shopping Center. From West Honolulu, take H1 east. After passing the Aloha Stadium, take the H3 exit to Kāne'ohe. Follow H3 to the very last exit.

COURSE Starting at the ʻAikahi Park Shopping Center at the corner of Kāneʻohe Bay Drive and Mōkapu Boulevard, turn right on Mōkapu Boulevard, and run in the direction of the mountains. Mōkapu Boulevard is a flat road with a wide shoulder. After Kalāheo High School, Mōkapu Boulevard becomes Mōkapu Saddle Road and soon begins a long, steep incline. At the top of the hill is a spectacular view of Kāneʻohe Bay as you head down the Kāneʻohe side of the saddle. Near the bottom of the hill, take the first right on Kāneʻohe Bay Drive. Kāneʻohe Bay Drive is a narrow, winding road with plenty of rolling hills. Continue along Kāneʻohe Bay Drive until you return to the starting point at ʻAikahi Park.

HIGHLIGHTS This course provides a balanced training run with a long hill, some rolling hills, long flat stretches, and some terrific views of Kāneʻohe Bay. You will not have to cross many intersections, so you can get into a comfortable long-distance rhythm. The sections of this loop with the heaviest traffic are also the stretches that have the widest shoulders, so the traffic doesn't come into play. You can easily stretch this course into a much longer run by adding an out-and-back leg along North Kalāheo Avenue, which will take you all the way out to Kailua Beach Park.

CAUTIONS As mentioned earlier, this route is dry and shadeless, so avoid running during the heat of the day. On the backside of the saddle road, the hill blocks much of the cooling trade winds, so heat can build up quickly. Along Kāneʻohe Bay Drive, the shoulder gets narrow in spots, so be very careful, and run facing the oncoming traffic.

ENCHANTED LAKES LOOP

DISTANCE: *2.9 or 6.1 miles (4.67 or 9.82 km)*
SURFACE: *Sidewalks and blacktop; flat*
SUITABLE FOR: *All levels*
LOCATION: *Windward Side (Map Region 3)*
COURSE: 🚶 🚶 🚶 🚶
PARKING: 🚶 🚶 🚶
AMENITIES: 🚶 🚶 🚶
SAFETY: 🚶 🚶 🚶 🚶
OVERALL RATING: 🚶 🚶 🚶 🚶

OVERVIEW Many neighborhood residents enjoy walking, running, and cycling this easy, relatively flat loop around the Enchanted Lakes subdivision of Kailua Town. To add a little spice to this loop, take a detour through the Norfolk division on the Old Kalaniana'ole Road, which will give a few hills and about 3 miles to your run. The Norfolk section is an underdeveloped neighborhood sprinkled with white picket fences and luxurious high-end homes. A rest room facility and a water fountain are at the Keolu Elementary School.

DIRECTIONS From Honolulu, take H1 to the Pali Highway (61). Follow the Pali Highway to Kailua. Turn right at the junction of Kalaniana'ole Highway (72). Turn left at the first traffic light onto Keolu Drive. Continue through the first traffic light, and turn into the parking lot of Keolu Elementary School.

COURSE Starting from the Keolu Elementary School, follow the Keolu Drive loop around the Enchanted Lake subdivision for a gentle, relatively flat 2.9-mile run. If you decide to add on the Norfolk portion, turn right out of the school parking lot, and turn left up the Kanapu'u Drive hill. Kanapu'u winds through the Kailua Bluffs neighborhood before ending at Kalaniana'ole Highway. Turn left on the highway, and when there is a break in the traffic, cross to

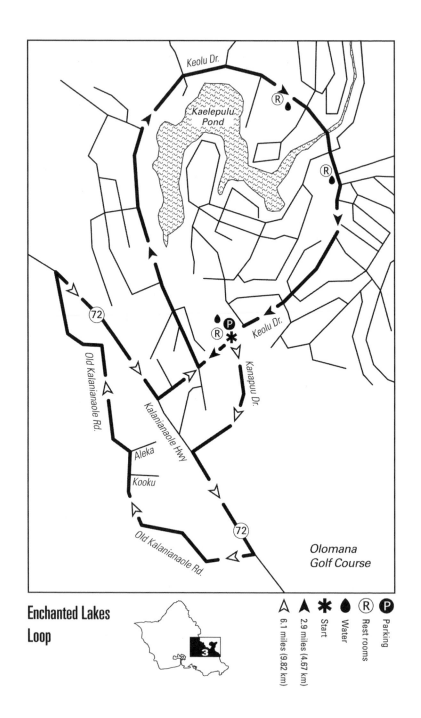

Keolu Dr.

Kaelepulu
Pond

Ⓡ

Ⓡ

Keolu Dr.

Ⓡ Ⓟ
✳

72

Kanapuu Dr.

Old Kalanianaole Rd.

Kalanianaole Hwy

Aleka

Kooku

Old Kalanianaole Rd.

72

Olomana
Golf Course

**Enchanted Lakes
Loop**

3

△ 6.1 miles (9.82 km)
▲ 2.9 miles (4.67 km)
✳ Start
● Water
Ⓡ Rest rooms
Ⓟ Parking

the opposite side, and continue toward Waimānalo. Take the first right on Old Kalaniana'ole Road. This section is nicely shaded with plenty of rolling hills. After 2 miles, you come back to the main highway. Turn right, cross back over Kalaniana'ole Highway, and continue back down to Keolu Drive. Turning left on Keolu, continue to the bottom of the hill, take another left, and follow the Keolu loop around Enchanted Lakes.

HIGHLIGHTS Kailua is the largest of the windward communities, and many of its residents are quite active. Although this course is not the most scenic, you never have to cross any intersections, so you can maintain a steady pace throughout your run. A number of other great courses are in Kailua, and you can match them up to make for longer runs. See the sections on Kailua Beach and Lanikai Loop, both of which can be added on to this loop run to add some distance if you get bored with running around in circles.

CAUTIONS The loop around Enchanted Lakes can get hot, so you should run in the early morning or early evening. If you choose to add the Norfolk portion of the run, please take care crossing Kalaniana'ole Highway. There are no pedestrian crosswalks at either of the cross points, and traffic can be moving fairly fast through this section.

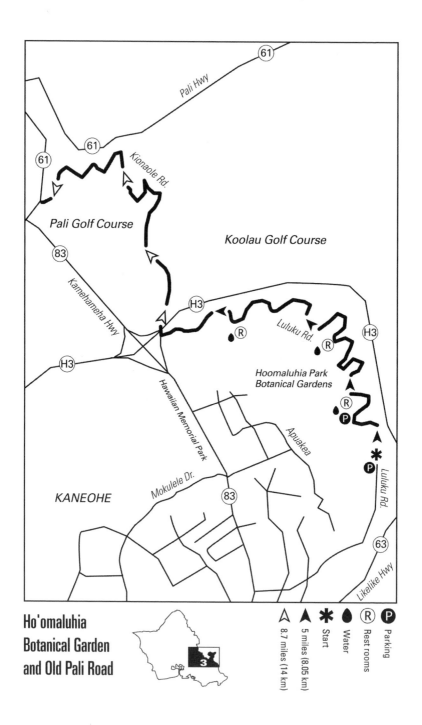

**Ho'omaluhia
Botanical Garden
and Old Pali Road**

8.7 miles (14 km)

5 miles (8.05 km)

Start

Water

Rest rooms

Parking

HOʻOMALUHIA
BOTANICAL GARDEN
AND OLD PALI ROAD

DISTANCE:	*5 or 8.7 miles (8.05 or 14 km)*
SURFACE:	*Blacktop; hilly*
SUITABLE FOR:	*All levels*
LOCATION:	*Windward Side (Map Region 3)*
COURSE:	卐 卐 卐 卐 卐
PARKING:	卐 卐 卐
AMENITIES:	卐 卐 卐
SAFETY:	卐 卐 卐 卐
OVERALL RATING:	卐 卐 卐 卐

OVERVIEW Hoʻomaluhia Botanical Garden is a 400-acre nature preserve maintained by the city and county of Honolulu. The garden is at the base of the Koʻolau Mountains, which provide a dramatic backdrop. This is a beautiful run along a paved road through lush tropical foliage. However, the entire course consists of rolling hills, so avoid this run if you want to keep your heart rate constant. The road through the garden is 2.5 miles, so an out-and-back run will give you a challenging 5-mile run. If you are up for more distance, simply walk around the fence at the far end of the garden, and continue to the Old Pali Road. This road has some light traffic until you pass the entrance to the Koʻolau Golf Course; at that point, the road is closed to cars, and you can enjoy this secluded old road without the fear of running into a car. The Old Pali Road ends at the Pali Highway (61). Turn around here, and head back for a challenging 8.7-mile run.

Rest rooms are available at the visitors' center, 1 mile in from the main gate. The center also has a water fountain, but you should bring your own supply if you plan on running the full 8.7-mile course. Rest rooms are also available in the clubhouse at the Koʻo-lau Golf Course.

DIRECTIONS From Honolulu, take H1 west to the Likelike Highway (63). Follow the Likelike Highway to Kāneʻohe. After passing through the Wilson Tunnel and emerging on the windward side, turn right at the second traffic light onto ʻAnoʻi Road. From ʻAnoʻi Road, turn right at the first stop sign on Luluku Road. Luluku Road will take you to the entrance gate of the garden. Park along the street just before the gate. This is a quiet residential neighborhood, so do not block any driveways, and keep the noise down if you are doing an early morning run.

COURSE Starting at the garden's entrance gate, simply follow the road for 2.5 miles of rolling hills until you reach the far end of the garden. The main gate does not open to vehicular traffic until 9 AM. If you arrive early, the entrance gate will be closed, but the park is open to walkers and joggers, so you can just walk around the gate. About 1 mile in on your left is a visitor's center that provides maps of the various trails that wind throughout the garden. If you want a change of pace, pick up a map, and take a detour on some of the trails. When you reach the end of the garden, you can hop the fence and continue on the Old Pali Road, or you can turn around and head back to the main gate for a hilly 5-mile run.

If you decide to take the full 8.7-mile run, after you hop the fence, follow the Old Pali Road across H3. This road will take you past the entrance of the Koʻolau Golf Course. About 0.25 mile past the golf course entrance, you will come to another fence where the Old Pali Road is closed to cars. Walk around the fence, and continue on this historic road, which was the original road that connected Honolulu to the windward side. It has been closed to traffic for quite some time but continues to be a popular running course. Take your time along this road, and enjoy the peaceful atmosphere. Near the end of this road, you will come to yet another fence. You can turn around at this point, or continue on for a short way where you meet up with the new Pali Highway. Turn around here, and retrace your steps to your start point at the main gate of the garden.

HIGHLIGHTS First and foremost is the lush tropical beauty of this park. You will see the spectacular Koʻolau Mountains throughout the run. The Koʻolau Golf Course is an interesting detour, if you want to get a firsthand look at the golf course that is rated the most difficult in the United States. As you continue past the golf course, you will run along the base of the Koʻolau Mountains and under the Pali Lookout, where in 1795 King Kamehameha fought the final battle for Oʻahu, defeating Oʻahu's ruling chief, Kalanikupule, allowing Kamehameha to conquer Oʻahu and unify the islands. Many of Kalanikupule's brave defenders were forced off these cliffs and fell to their deaths at the base of the Pali.

CAUTIONS This is a hilly course, so do not go out too fast. The course is best enjoyed at a more casual pace. There are no street-lights, either in the garden or along the Old Pali Road, so run here during the daylight hours only. If you choose to run in the early evening hours, be aware that it gets dark much sooner on the wind-ward side. As mentioned above, the Old Pali Road along the base of the Koʻolaus was the final dramatic resting place for many brave Hawaiian warriors, so you might want to take that into consideration if you choose to run through there at night. This sacred area must be respected at all times.

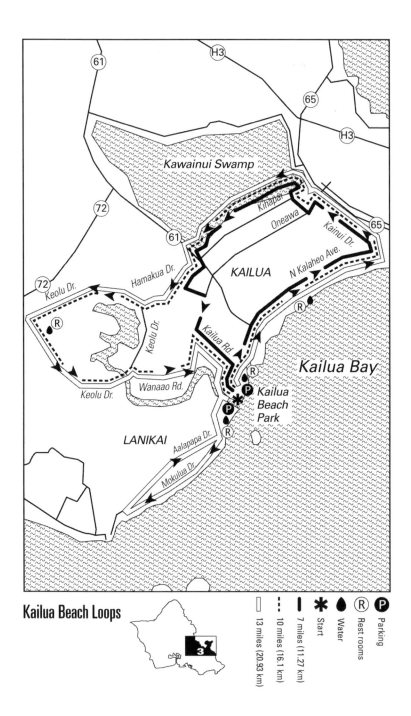

Kailua Beach Loops

3

▯	13 miles (20.93 km)
⫶	10 miles (16.1 km)
▮	7 miles (11.27 km)
✳	Start
⬤	Water
Ⓡ	Rest rooms
ⓟ	Parking

KAILUA BEACH LOOPS

DISTANCE: *7, 10, or 13 miles (11.27, 16.1, or 20.93 km)*
SURFACE: *Sand, blacktop, sidewalks, and bike paths; flat*
SUITABLE FOR: *All levels*
LOCATION: *Windward Side (Map Region 3)*
COURSE: 🏃 🏃 🏃
PARKING: 🏃 🏃 🏃 🏃
AMENITIES: 🏃 🏃 🏃 🏃
SAFETY: 🏃 🏃 🏃
OVERALL RATING: 🏃 🏃 🏃 🏃

OVERVIEW This route offers many different lengths and surfaces. Options include a beautiful 2.5-mile stretch of Kailua Beach, majestic palm tree–lined roads, and a levee bordering Hawai'i's largest freshwater wetlands. Kailua Beach Park offers free parking, public rest rooms, and water fountains.

DIRECTIONS From Honolulu, take the Pali Highway (61) directly into Kailua Town. Continue straight through town to North Kalāheo Avenue. Turn right on North Kalāheo for a short distance before turning left at the Kalapawai Market, entering the Kailua Beach Park.

COURSE For the 7-mile course, run north along the beach starting at the Kailua Beach Park. When the beach begins to narrow, look for one of the many public access paths that lead to North Kalāheo Avenue. Turn right on North Kalāheo, and continue in the same northerly direction. Turn left on Kainui Drive, and follow this beautiful tree-lined road to the traffic light at Oneawa Street. Turn left on Oneawa for one block, and take a right on Kaha. Follow Kaha to a small park, where you pick up an access road to the Kawainui Marsh Levee. Follow the levee along the perimeter of this natural wetland. At the end of the levee, follow the road up to the Pali Highway (also known as Kailua Road), and turn left, heading back into

Kailua Town. At the first traffic light, turn right onto Hāmākua Drive. Take a left at the next traffic light (Hahani), and follow Hahani to Kailua Road. Turn right on Kailua Road. Kailua Road makes a sharp left at the first traffic light. Take that left, and continue down Kailua Road until you reach North Kalāheo. Cross North Kalāheo, and enter Kailua Beach Park.

For the 10-mile course, continue along Hāmākua Drive. At the end of Hāmākua, turn right on Keolu Drive. Keolu Drive makes a large loop around the Enchanted Lakes subdivision. Follow Keolu around Enchanted Lakes. Before completing the entire circle, take a right on Wanaao Road. Continue on Wanaao as it bends to the left. At the first traffic light, turn right on Kailua Road. Follow Kailua Road to North Kalāheo. Turn right at North Kalāheo, and follow it around to the back entrance of Kailua Beach Park, which is the end of the 10-mile course. If you are just warming up, continue past the beach park, cross the canal bridge, and head for Lanikai.

For the 13-mile course, continue past Kailua Beach Park, take a left at the stop sign, and follow the road up a short hill into the exclusive Lanikai neighborhood. As you enter Lanikai, stay to the left, and follow the Lanikai loop road in a clockwise direction. After one 2.4-mile loop of Lanikai, continue back to the Kailua Beach starting point.

HIGHLIGHTS Consistently rated one of the top five beaches in the world, the 3-mile-long, crescent-shaped Kailua Beach offers soft white sand and extremely safe swimming. Kailua Beach is also a windsurfing mecca with the steady trade winds providing the perfect combination of offshore winds and minimal wave action. If you are interested in the local history, the vast Kawainui Marsh was once a fishpond big enough to support a large Hawaiian population. As the Hawaiian population dwindled in the 1800s, the pond was abandoned, and Chinese rice farmers took over. Rice proved to be unprofitable, and again these lowlands were abandoned until the 1920s, when a local sugar plantation began pumping the water out of the marsh to irrigate their fields. As Kailua Town began to develop, it was necessary to build a levee to prevent flooding, and the levee now offers a welcome diversion and incredible scenery along this particular running course.

CAUTIONS This is a safe run, but the course tends to get hot by midday, especially in the Enchanted Lakes area. Although beach running is picturesque, you should limit it to short distances, especially if you are prone to hip or Achilles tendon problems. The soft sand lacks stability and may cause excessive stretching of the Achilles tendon. Kailua Beach is extremely popular, and parking is limited, so arrive early to ensure a parking spot.

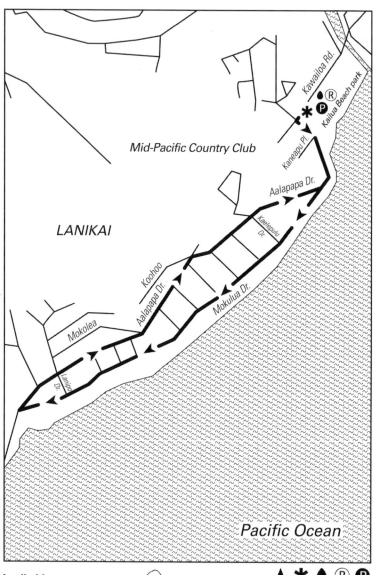

Mid-Pacific Country Club

LANIKAI

Kawailoa Rd.

Kailua Beach park

Kaneapu Pl.

Aalapapa Dr.

Kaelepulu Dr.

Koohoo

Aalapapa Dr.

Mokulua Dr.

Mokolea

Lanipo Dr.

Pacific Ocean

Lanikai Loop

 ✳ Ⓡ Ⓟ

2.4 miles (3.94 km)   Start   Water   Rest rooms   Parking

LANIKAI LOOP

DISTANCE:	*2.4 miles (3.94 km)*
SURFACE:	*Blacktop and bike path; flat, with gentle hills*
SUITABLE FOR:	*All levels*
LOCATION:	*Windward Side (Map Region 3)*
COURSE:	🏃 🏃 🏃 🏃
PARKING:	🏃 🏃 🏃
AMENITIES:	🏃 🏃
SAFETY:	🏃 🏃 🏃 🏃 🏃
OVERALL RATING:	🏃 🏃 🏃 🏃

OVERVIEW Lanikai is an exclusive beach neighborhood in Kailua. This beautiful cul-de-sac offers a quiet and safe running loop lined with a clearly defined bike path lane and shade trees. Parking, rest rooms, and water fountains are available just prior to entering Lanikai at the Kailua Beach Park. Lanikai itself does not offer any public rest rooms and has limited parking options.

DIRECTIONS From Honolulu, take the Pali Highway (61) directly into Kailua Town. Continue straight through town to North Kalāheo Avenue. Turn right on North Kalāheo, and continue past the Kailua Beach Park. At the stop sign, turn left, and follow the road up a short hill, around Alāla Point, and down into Lanikai. At the bottom of the hill, stay to the right, as the two roads that make up this loop are one-way running in a counterclockwise direction. Parking is limited to the side streets connecting the loop roads, so park outside Lanikai at or around Kailua Beach Park, and run the short 0.25 mile into Lanikai.

COURSE The Lanikai Loop consists of two one-way roads, 'A'alapapa Drive entering and Mokulua Drive exiting, that flow in a counterclockwise pattern. As always, you should run facing the traffic, so run this loop clockwise. The lower road, Mokulua, is flat and fronts the multimillion-dollar beachfront properties. At the far end of Lanikai, the road makes a sharp turn to the right and becomes ʻAʻalapapa Drive. ʻAʻalapapa offers a gentle change of pace with a number of small, rolling hills.

HIGHLIGHTS Developed in the mid-1920s as an exclusive and private getaway for wealthy Oʻahu families, Lanikai has long been a favorite with actors, artists, and professional athletes. Separated from the larger Kailua Beach to the north by a brief outcropping of rocks, Alāla Point, Lanikai Beach has also enjoyed consistently high rankings as a world-renowned beach. The entire length of Lanikai Beach is lined with multimillion-dollar homes but is easily accessible through numerous public beach access paths. A walking and jogging trail stretches along the Kaʻiwa Ridge bordering Lanikai, offering a spectacular view of this exclusive neighborhood. The trailhead is located off Kaʻelepulu Drive opposite the entrance to the Mid-Pacific Country Club.

CAUTIONS Despite the presence of a bike and jogging lane around the entire Lanikai loop, the loop is heavily traveled, with walkers, bikers, skateboarders, and in-line skaters. There are also many blind driveways and intersections. If you are running against traffic, be alert to cars exiting driveways, for they may be only looking for cars coming in the opposite direction. As mentioned above, parking is limited, so park outside and run into Lanikai.

PALI AND
MAUNAWILI TRAIL

DISTANCE:	*Up to 10 miles (16.1 km)*
SURFACE:	*Trail; moderate to steep hills*
SUITABLE FOR:	*All levels*
LOCATION:	*Windward Side (Map Region 3)*
COURSE:	🏃 🏃 🏃 🏃 🏃
PARKING:	🏃 🏃 🏃
AMENITIES:	🏃
SAFETY:	🏃 🏃 🏃
OVERALL RATING:	🏃 🏃 🏃 🏃

OVERVIEW Possibly the finest running trail on Oʻahu, this course was created by the Sierra Club and is very well maintained. The Pali and Maunawili Trail winds its way along the base of the spectacular Koʻolau Mountain range and provides great scenic vistas throughout. The trail is approximately 10 miles in length from the Pali Highway to Waimānalo. It offers some hilly sections, but the hills are relatively short and manageable. Numerous switchbacks provide tremendous views of windward Oʻahu. While running on trails, you will tend to concentrate on the ground in front of you because exposed roots and jutting rocks can quickly bring you to your knees if you don't pay attention. However, you cannot fully appreciate this run unless you take the time to look up occasionally and soak up the majestic and rugged Koʻolau Ridge that borders this trail.

The standard weather pattern in Hawaiʻi brings a great deal of precipitation to this area, especially in the winter months, so you should use trail shoes for improved footing. Even during the drier summer season, the trail may be muddy in sections; assume your shoes and lower legs will get muddy, and bring a change of shoes for after the run.

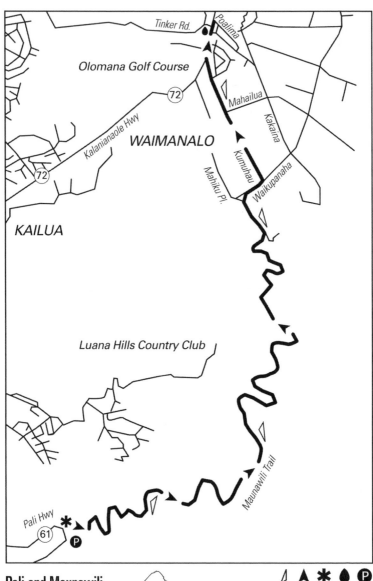

Tinker Rd.

Poalima

Olomana Golf Course

Mahailua

72

Kakaina

Kalanianaole Hwy

WAIMANALO

Mahiku Pl.

Kumuhau

Waikupanaha

72

KAILUA

Luana Hills Country Club

Maunawili Trail

Pali Hwy

61

Pali and Maunawili Trail

3

Return

Up to 10 miles (16.1 km)

Start

Water

Parking

DIRECTIONS From Honolulu, take the Pali Highway (61) to Kailua. After passing through the twin Pali Tunnels, stay in the right lane. About 0.25 mile past the tunnels, the Pali Highway makes a sharp horseshoe turn to the left. Midway through this turn is an exit to a scenic viewpoint parking area, where you will park. The trailhead is a short walk above the parking area. From Kailua or Kāneʻohe, take the Pali Highway Honolulu-bound. Pass the scenic viewpoint parking area on the left, and continue through the tunnels for about 1 mile. Take a right at the side road leading to the Pali Lookout. This road will wind its way back to the Pali Lookout parking area. Continue through the parking area, and follow the signs to Kailua. You will merge back onto the Pali Highway heading for Kailua. Stay in the right lane through the tunnels, and take the scenic viewpoint exit into the parking area.

COURSE The most common strategy for running this trail is to park at the Pali end and select a time that you would like to run. Run in for a set amount of minutes, then turn around, and return to the starting point at the parking area. This trail lends itself well to an out-and-back run. If you are running with a group, another option is to leave one car at the Waimānalo end of the trail and run the entire length. Ten miles of trail running takes longer than the equivalent number of miles on the road, so if you plan to run the full length, expect it to take more time than a standard 10-mile road run.

HIGHLIGHTS This trail brings you in touch with the splendors of a natural and unspoiled tropical rain forest on Oʻahu. The green, razor-sharp ridges that make up the Koʻolau Mountains of windward Oʻahu are unique in their splendor. This relatively new trail was developed in 1991, and, despite the heavy rainfall in this area, the trail remains in good running condition throughout the year. At many points along the trail, you will find spectacular views of the windward communities of Kailua and Waimānalo and the impressive twin peaks of the 1,640-foot Mount Olomana.

CAUTIONS First and foremost, you should lock your car, and do not leave behind anything of value. The scenic point parking area is known for break-ins. If you choose to run the full length of the trail, leave your car in a safe public parking area in Waimānalo Town rather than at the secluded trail end. Leaving your car in Waimā-nalo Town will add an extra 1.5 miles to your run, but the added security is well worth the trouble. If you park your car at the Waimā-nalo end of the trail, park at the Waimānalo Shopping Center, next to the Jack in the Box restaurant.

Plus, this trail can stay wet year-round, so use running shoes specifically designed for off-road running whenever attempting this trail. As with all secluded trail runs, do not run alone, and be sure to bring a supply of water. The humidity tends to be high along this tropical trail, and you will need to replenish your fluids often. Finally, the Pali and Maunawili Trail is often used by mountain bikers and hikers, so be cautious when approaching blind corners.

TEMPLE VALLEY AND KĀNE'OHE BAY

DISTANCE:	*8.2-mile loop (13.2 km)*
SURFACE:	*Blacktop; rolling hills*
SUITABLE FOR:	*Intermediate to advanced*
LOCATION:	*Windward Side (Map Region 3)*
COURSE:	🏃 🏃 🏃
PARKING:	🏃 🏃 🏃 🏃
AMENITIES:	🏃 🏃
SAFETY:	🏃 🏃 🏃
OVERALL RATING:	🏃 🏃 🏃

OVERVIEW Parts of this 8.2-mile route along Kamehameha Highway are very scenic as it winds along the shoreline of Kāne'ohe Bay. The loop has wide shoulders along Kahekili Highway and narrow to nonexistent shoulders along some stretches of Kamehameha Highway. Rest rooms and drinks are available at the McDonalds and the Times Super Market in the Ko'olau Shopping Center. Rest rooms and water fountains are also at the He'eia Elementary School and the Kāne'ohe Fishing Pier.

DIRECTIONS From Honolulu, take Likelike Highway (63) to Kāne'ohe. After the Wilson Tunnel, take the first exit, Kahekili Highway (83). After 1 mile, Kahekili narrows to a two-lane road. Turn right at the first traffic light (Hui Iwa Street) after the road narrows. Park in the Ko'olau Shopping Center parking lot.

COURSE From the McDonalds, turn left on Kahekili Highway. The course starts out with some long, rolling hills to help you get warmed up. Stay on the left side of the road, facing traffic. Turn left at Ha'ikū Road, and continue along the sidewalk, passing He'eia Elementary School and Windward Mall on your right. Turn left on Kamehameha Highway and continue to run on the left along a

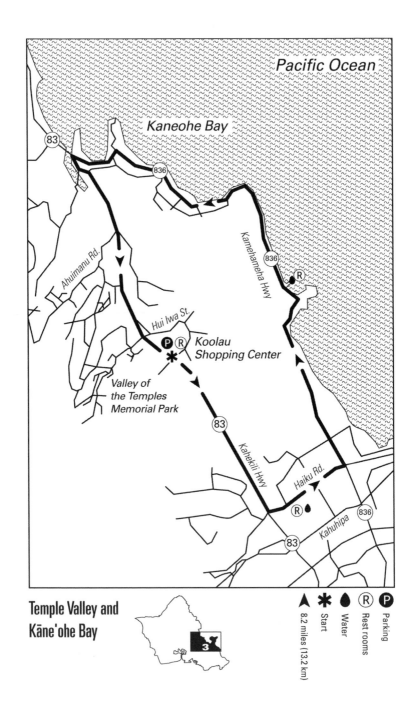

Pacific Ocean

Kaneohe Bay

83

836

Ahuimanu Rd.

Kamehameha Hwy

836

R

Hui Iwa St.

P R   Koolau
Shopping Center

Valley of
the Temples
Memorial Park

83

Kahekili Hwy

Haiku Rd.

R

R ●

Kahuhipa

836

83

Temple Valley and
Kāne'ohe Bay

3

▲ 8.2 miles (13.2 km)   ✳ Start   ● Water   Ⓡ Rest rooms   Ⓟ Parking

paved pathway. After passing King Intermediate School, you will pass through a mangrove forest and cross the He'eia Stream Bridge before a short climb to the He'eia State Park. Here the road curves to the left, drops down to the shoreline, and begins a long stretch along the picturesque Kāne'ohe Bay. Kamehameha Highway eventually merges with Kahekili Highway in Kahalu'u at the Hygienic Store. At this point, turn left again, and head back along Kahekili Highway, completing the loop at the Ko'olau Shopping Center.

HIGHLIGHTS Across the street from the shopping center is Valley of the Temples cemetery, where the former Philippine president Ferdinand Marcos was temporarily housed after his death, following his forced departure from the Philippines. This is also the site for the Byodo-In Temple. This temple was built in 1968 in memory of the first Japanese immigrants to settle in Hawai'i and is a replica of a famous 900-year-old Buddhist temple in Uji, Japan. The grounds surrounding the temple include well-manicured gardens, a reflection pool, and a variety of wildlife, including numerous peacocks. If you decide to run through the cemetery to check out the impressive temple, please stay on the roadway and respect this sacred ground. The best bet is to drive in after your run, so you can take a camera. No matter what the weather, the Byodo-In makes for tremendous photo opportunities.

The He'eia State Park is a small, undeveloped park that is best known as a scenic park overlooking the He'eia fishpond, one of the few remaining fishponds in Kāne'ohe Bay that in ancient times contained an 88-acre fish farm. Where Kamehameha Highway merges with Kahekili Highway are a gas station and the Hygienic Store, and behind the gas station is the Kahalu'u fishpond. This fishpond was used in the filming of *Karate Kid II* as a backdrop for a small Okinawan fishing village. It is now the site of a chapel used for O'ahu's popular wedding industry.

CAUTIONS The few areas of concern are along the narrow, winding stretch of Kamehameha Highway because of the sections that have little or no shoulder. Stay on the left, and be careful around some of the blind turns. Parking is plentiful at the Ko'olau Shopping Center for morning runs, but due to heavy theater traffic, parking may be limited in the evening hours.

WINDWARD COAST

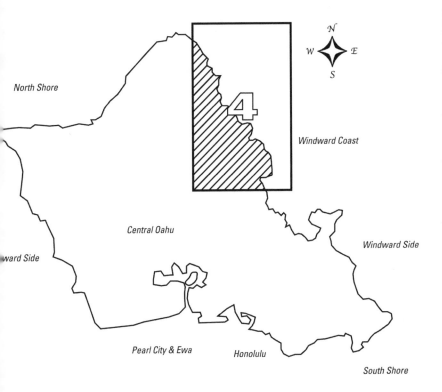

North Shore

4

Windward Coast

Central Oahu

Windward Side

ward Side

Pearl City & Ewa

Honolulu

South Shore

N

W   E

S

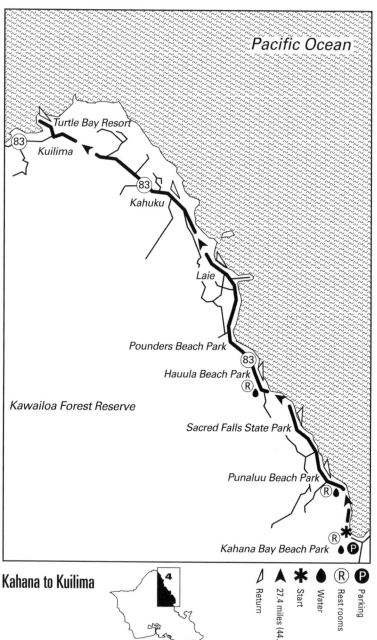

Pacific Ocean

Turtle Bay Resort

83

Kuilima

83

Kahuku

Laie

Pounders Beach Park

83

Hauula Beach Park

Ⓡ

Kawailoa Forest Reserve

Sacred Falls State Park

Punaluu Beach Park

Ⓡ

Ⓡ

Kahana Bay Beach Park

Ⓟ

Kahana to Kuilima

4

 27.4 miles (44.1 km)

Return

Start

Water

Ⓡ Rest rooms

Ⓟ Parking

KAHANA TO KUILIMA

<table>
<tr><td>DISTANCE:</td><td>Medium to long out-and-back course, up to 27.4 miles (44.1 km)</td></tr>
</table>

DISTANCE: *Medium to long out-and-back course, up to 27.4 miles (44.1 km)*

(All distances listed below are out-and-back.)

KAHANA BAY

— *to Punaluʻu Beach Park = 3.7 miles (5.95 km)*

— *to Sacred Falls = 6.3 miles (10.14 km)*

— *to Hauʻula Beach Park = 9.7 miles (15.61 km)*

— *to Pounders Beach Park = 14.62 miles (23.53 km)*

— *to Lāʻie = 15.8 miles (25.43 km)*

— *to Kahuku = 20.82 miles (33.52 km)*

— *to Kuilima (Turtle Bay Resort) = 27.4 miles (44.1 km)*

SURFACE: *Blacktop and coastline road; relatively flat, some small rolling hills*

SUITABLE FOR: *All levels*

LOCATION: *Windward Coast (Map Region 4)*

COURSE: (4)

PARKING: (3)

AMENITIES: (4)

SAFETY: (3)

OVERALL RATING: (4)

OVERVIEW This single stretch of two-lane highway borders the ocean on Oʻahu's spectacular windward coast, which faces the Pacific trade winds, resulting in breezier and cooler weather. The entire length out and back is just over 27 miles, but you can choose from a variety of turnaround or starting points to create the desired distance. Traffic can get heavy, but the shoulders are mostly wide enough to provide a safe buffer. This course is primarily flat with many public beach parks along the way that provide rest rooms and water.

DIRECTIONS From Honolulu, take H1 to the Likelike Highway (63) exit. Take Likelike Highway Kāneʻohe-bound. After passing through the Wilson Tunnel to the windward side, take the first exit onto Kahekili Highway (83). After approximately 4.3 miles, Kahekili merges with Kamehameha Highway and continues north along the coast. Kahana Bay Beach Park is 10 miles north of where the Kahekili and Kamehameha Highways merge.

From leeward Oʻahu, take H1 to the H3 and Kāneʻohe exit. After passing through the tunnels, take the first Kāneʻohe exit. After exiting, stay in the far right lane as you merge with Likelike Highway, which will take you right onto Kahekili Highway. Once on Kahekili, follow the directions listed above.

COURSE On this versatile out-and-back course, you can choose your desired distance and pick the starting point and turnaround point to meet your needs. Since it follows the shoreline, this stretch is almost entirely flat. Traveling north along this coastal road will take you through numerous small towns and past a variety of white sand beaches. After you pass Pounders Beach Park, the road leaves the coast, traveling inland past the Polynesian Cultural Center, Lāʻie, and Kahuku. After Kahuku, the shoulder widens, and the road straightens as the surrounding landscape switches to open farm fields on the left and shrimp and prawn farms on the right. The final stretch skirts along the perimeter of the Links at Kuilima golf course, a classic links golf course designed by Arnold Palmer. At the entrance to the Turtle Bay Resort, turn right off the highway, and continue along the resort access road. The road ends at the resort's lobby, which has an attractive public access lagoon to the right.

HIGHLIGHTS This course offers many stretches of white sand beach intermingled with quaint little country towns. Points of interest along the way include the Sacred Falls trail that extends back into Kaluanui Valley. This trail is now closed to the public after a severe rock fall in 1999 caused several deaths to hikers. The Polynesian Cultural Center is open Monday through Saturday and provides an opportunity to learn firsthand about the various South Pacific cultures. The town of Lāʻie is the home of Brigham Young University's Hawaiʻi campus and the Mormon Temple of the Pacific. Just past the town of Kahuku is a large active shrimp farm where you can purchase freshly harvested shrimp and prawns from a roadside stand.

CAUTIONS As Kamehameha Highway winds along the shoreline, this two-lane road offers minimal shoulders, so you should run facing the traffic. As with many of the more secluded public beaches, you should be careful not to leave valuables in your car.

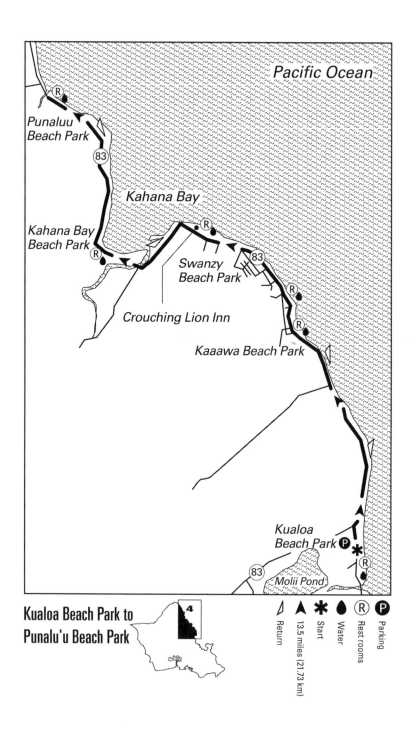

Pacific Ocean

Punaluu
Beach Park

83

Kahana Bay

Kahana Bay
Beach Park

Swanzy
Beach Park

Crouching Lion Inn

83

Kaaawa Beach Park

Kualoa
Beach Park Ⓟ

Molii Pond

83

**Kualoa Beach Park to
Punalu'u Beach Park**

Return · 13.5 miles (21.73 km) · Start · Water · Ⓡ Rest rooms · Ⓟ Parking

KUALOA BEACH PARK TO PUNALU'U BEACH PARK

DISTANCE:	*Medium to long out-and-back course, up to 13.5 miles (21.73 km)*
	(All distances listed below are out-and-back.)
	KUALOA
	—to Ka'a'awa Beach Park = 5.2 miles (8.37 km)
	—to Swanzy Beach Park = 6.5 miles (10.46 km)
	—to Crouching Lion Inn = 8.0 miles (12.88 km)
	—to Kahana Bay Beach Park = 9.9 miles (15.93 km)
	—to Punalu'u Beach Park = 13.5 miles (21.73 km)
SURFACE:	*Blacktop and coastline road; relatively flat, some mild rolling hills*
SUITABLE FOR:	*All levels*
LOCATION:	*Windward Coast (Map Region 4)*
COURSE:	⚜ ⚜ ⚜ ⚜ ⚜
PARKING:	⚜ ⚜ ⚜
AMENITIES:	⚜ ⚜ ⚜ ⚜
SAFETY:	⚜ ⚜
OVERALL RATING:	⚜ ⚜ ⚜ ⚜

OVERVIEW This flexible run can be as long or as short as you want. Winding its way along the spectacular windward coast, this course starts at Kualoa Beach Park and follows Kamehameha Highway (83). This course is never more than a few feet from the ocean and has the benefit of many beach parks along the way that offer rest room facilities, water fountains, and showers. Of course, if you get a little overheated, what better way to cool off than a quick dip in the ocean? There are also no major intersection crossings, so it is perfect for a long, slow training run.

DIRECTIONS As for the Kahana to Kuilima run, from Honolulu, take H1 to the Likelike Highway (63) exit. Take Likelike Highway Kāneʻohe-bound. After passing through the Wilson Tunnel to the windward side, take the first exit onto Kahekili Highway (83). After approximately 4.3 miles, Kahekili merges with Kamehameha Highway and continues north along the coast. The entrance to Kualoa Beach Park is on the right, approximately 5.4 miles from where Kahekili and Kamehameha Highways merge.

From leeward Oʻahu, take H1 to the H3 and Kāneʻohe exit. After passing through the tunnels, take the first Kāneʻohe exit. After exiting, stay in the far right lane as you merge with Likelike Highway, which will take you right onto Kahekili Highway. Once on Kahekili, follow the directions listed above.

COURSE On this route, you will constantly pinch yourself to make sure you are not dreaming. Not many places in the world are more attractive than this coastal road. Parking is plentiful at the Kualoa Beach Park, but, as with most of these isolated areas, you should not leave valuables in your car. From the park, head north along the coast. Decide beforehand how many minutes out you want to go, and try to stick with it. Relatively flat but never boring, this route is hypnotic in its beauty, and you can very easily get carried away.

HIGHLIGHTS The major highlight is the course itself. You will encounter one small white sand beach after another, and the air is clean and stimulating. When you first start out, you will see the entrance to Kualoa Ranch on your left. This ranch is open to the public and offers numerous activities, including horseback rides deep into the spectacular Kaʻaʻawa Valley. The ranch was the filming location for the original *Jurassic Park*. Some other movies filmed in Kaʻaʻawa Valley include *Godzilla*, *Windtalkers*, *Mighty Joe Young*, and *George of the Jungle*.

Just past the ranch entrance are the ruins of the Old Kualoa Sugar Mill, the last remains of the sugar industry on the windward coast. At the Crouching Lion Inn, stop for a few seconds, and check out the crouching lion rock formation on the ridge behind the restaurant.

Beyond the Crouching Lion Inn, you will come to Kahana Bay and the 5,300-acre Kahana Valley State Park. Kahana Valley was the site of a large Hawaiian population during ancient times and has been established as a "cultural living park" open to visitors. Trails extend deep into this historic valley and offer an excellent glimpse into the ancient lifestyles of the Hawaiians who inhabited this lush valley.

CAUTIONS Kamehameha Highway is a two-lane, winding road that is the sole connecting route for the people living along the windward coast. This route is popular with tourists, too, so traffic may be heavy at times. The shoulder gets narrow in sections, especially on the numerous little bridges you will encounter. This is also a popular route for bicyclists on weekend mornings, so stay alert.

The prevailing weather conditions along the coast include trade winds blowing off the ocean. These winds can be cooling, especially during the hotter summer months, but they can be brisk, and they also bring periodic rainsqualls. The squalls, at times, can be intense, but they tend to be short and refreshing, especially during extra-long training runs. After your turnaround, you will find that the trade winds are now head winds. Although these winds are refreshing, gusting trades can also pick up some sand from the neighboring beaches.

NORTH SHORE

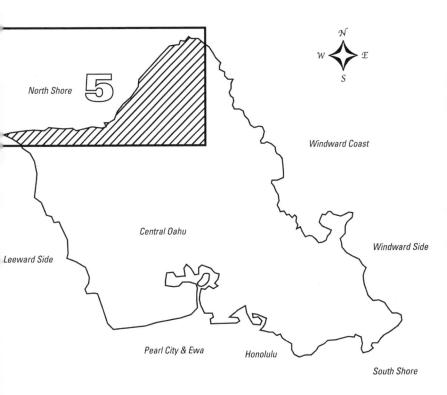

North Shore

Windward Coast

Central Oahu

Leeward Side

Windward Side

Pearl City & Ewa

Honolulu

South Shore

N
W *E*
S

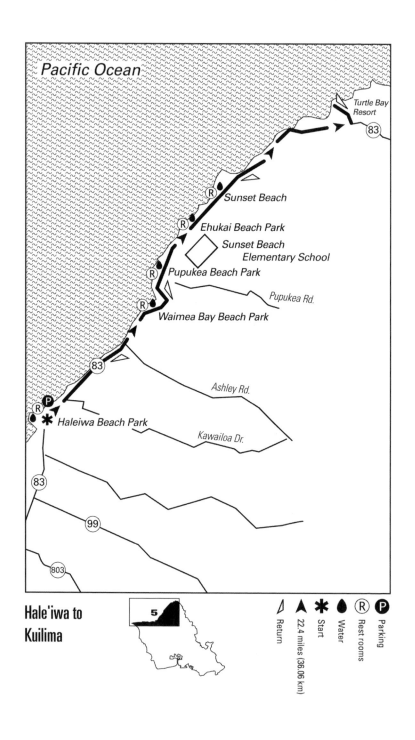

Pacific Ocean

Turtle Bay Resort

83

R Sunset Beach

R Ehukai Beach Park

Sunset Beach Elementary School

R Pupukea Beach Park

Pupukea Rd.

R Waimea Bay Beach Park

83

Ashley Rd.

R P

* Haleiwa Beach Park

Kawailoa Dr.

83

99

803

Hale'iwa to Kuilima

5

Return | 22.4 miles (36.06 km) | Start | Water | R Rest rooms | P Parking

HALEʻIWA TO KUILIMA

DISTANCE: *Medium to long out-and-back course, up to 22.4 miles (36.06 km) (All distances listed below are out-and-back.)*

HALEʻIWA

— to Waimea Bay = 8 miles (12.88 km)

— to Pūpūkea (Shark's Cove) = 9.6 miles (15.46 km)

— to Sunset Beach Elementary (ʻEhukai Beach Park) = 12.2 miles (19.64 km)

— to Sunset Beach = 14.2 miles (22.86 km)

— to Kuilima (Turtle Bay Resort entrance) = 21.4 miles (34.45 km)

— to Kuilima (Turtle Bay Resort lobby) = 22.4 miles (36.06 km)

SURFACE: *Blacktop; mostly flat*

SUITABLE FOR: *Intermediate to advanced*

LOCATION: *North Shore (Map Region 5)*

COURSE: 🏃 🏃 🏃 🏃

PARKING: 🏃 🏃 🏃

AMENITIES: 🏃 🏃 🏃 🏃

SAFETY: 🏃 🏃 🏃

OVERALL RATING: 🏃 🏃 🏃 🏃

OVERVIEW From the Haleʻiwa Beach Park to the Turtle Bay Resort at Kuilima, this out-and-back course follows Kamehameha Highway (83) along Oʻahu's north shore. This two-lane road is heavily traveled, but it has a wide shoulder. Be sure to run facing traffic. Between Haleʻiwa and Kuilima, a number of beach parks offer public rest rooms and water fountains, and they make for good turnaround spots depending on the distance you want to run. This course is good for distance training because it has few intersections to cross. The prevailing trade winds will be in your face while you run from Haleʻiwa, but they will be at your back on the return run.

DIRECTIONS From Honolulu, take H1 west. After bypassing Pearl City on H1, stay in the right lane, and take H2 north. From H2, take the Wahiawā exit. Continue straight through Wahiawā, following signs to Hale'iwa. Pass through the pineapple fields and the Dole Plantation, and head down a 6-mile hill. At the base of the hill, take a left at the traffic light. Enter a traffic circle (Weed Junction), and take the first right off the circle. Follow Kamehameha Highway (83) through the town of Hale'iwa. After you pass over the historic Hale'iwa Bridge, the entrance to the Hale'iwa Beach Park will be 0.3 mile away on the left.

From Kāne'ohe or Kailua, take H3 to the H1 west Pearl City junction. Take H1 west, and follow the directions above. From west O'ahu, take H1 east past Waikele. Take exit 8B east onto H2 north.

COURSES Exit the Hale'iwa Beach Park, heading northeast away from Hale'iwa. At the traffic light, turn left. Continue along Kamehameha Highway. The first turnaround will be at 4 miles at the entrance to the Waimea Bay Beach Park. Continuing on for another 1.6 miles will take you around the perimeter of Waimea Bay and bring you to the Pūpūkea Beach Park, where you will find a Foodland, in case you want to grab a cold sports drink. After another 2.6 miles along the highway, you will arrive at Sunset Beach Elementary School and 'Ehukai Beach Park, the site of the world-famous Banzai Pipeline surf break. One mile past the school and the beach park is Sunset Beach. The out-and-back trip to Sunset Beach is 14.2 miles. If you are in the final stages of your marathon training and need to get in an extra-long run, continue to the entrance of the Turtle Bay Resort at Kuilima for 21.4 miles out-and-back. To gain an extra mile, you can also pass the Turtle Bay Resort entrance and run to the lobby.

HIGHLIGHTS O'ahu's north shore abounds with natural beauty. Waimea Bay is one of the most famous big-wave surfing sites in the world, with winter waves cresting up to 35 feet. Waimea Bay is a horseshoe-shaped cove that provides tremendous viewpoints both as you enter and exit the area. Pūpūkea Beach Park's Shark's Cove offers the best north shore scuba diving and snorkeling during the summer months. Don't worry—Shark's Cove is named for an underwater rock formation and is quite safe. The next stop is the Banzai Pipeline surf break just to the left of 'Ehukai Beach Park. Undoubtedly, the Banzai Pipeline provides the best spot for viewing big wave surfing. Unlike most surf spots where the waves tend to break far offshore, the Pipeline's famous clean tubular break is within a few hundred yards of the beach. The large surf breaks occur in the winter months. During the summer months, the powerful north shore surf disappears, and the water becomes calm and smooth, offering some of the best snorkeling and scuba diving on O'ahu. The Turtle Bay Resort at Kuilima has been transformed into a world-class resort, offering two championship golf courses, miles of jogging trails, and spectacular coastline.

CAUTIONS Traffic is always heavy along this two-lane highway. The large waves of the winter months attract multitudes of both locals and tourists to marvel at this natural phenomenon. During the summer months, the waves flatten out, and the scuba divers and snorkelers flock to the region. When the surf is big, be especially careful around the beach parks, as cars are constantly pulling in and out of the parking areas. This route is not recommended after dark because streetlights are limited, and there are long, unlit stretches of road. During the winter months, stay out of the water at all of these beach parks. Even if the waves are not particularly large, strong rip currents can make swimming hazardous. If you need to cool off, use one of the showers located at the beach parks, and leave the ocean to the experienced surfers.

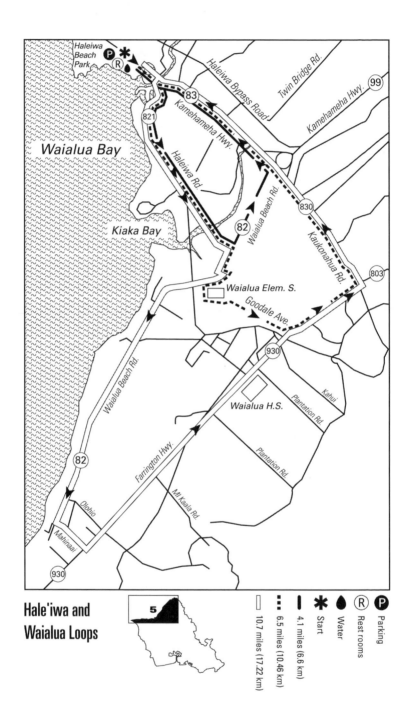

Hale'iwa and
Waialua Loops

HALE'IWA AND WAIALUA LOOPS

DISTANCE:	*4.1, 6.5, or 10.7 miles (6.6, 10.46, or 17.22 km)*
SURFACE:	*Blacktop; flat*
SUITABLE FOR:	*All levels*
LOCATION:	*North Shore (Map Region 5)*
COURSE:	🩴 🩴 🩴 🩴
PARKING:	🩴 🩴 🩴
AMENITIES:	🩴 🩴 🩴
SAFETY:	🩴 🩴 🩴
OVERALL RATING:	🩴 🩴 🩴

OVERVIEW These three loops of varying distances start from the parking area of the Hale'iwa Beach Park, which provides ample free parking, public rest rooms, showers, and water fountains. These courses are flat and provide some good views of the picturesque north shore and the Hale'iwa Boat Harbor. These courses tend to get hot during midday, but the ocean breezes can make even afternoon runs bearable. Streetlights are limited in this area, so avoid running after dark.

DIRECTIONS As for the Hale'iwa to Kuilima course, from Honolulu, take H1 west. After bypassing Pearl City on H1, stay in the right lane, and take H2 north. From H2, take the Wahiawā exit. Continue straight through Wahiawā, following signs to Hale'iwa. Pass through the pineapple fields and the Dole Plantation, and head down a 6-mile hill. At the base of the hill, take a left at the traffic light. Enter a traffic circle (Weed Junction), and take the first right off the circle. Follow Kamehameha Highway (83) through the town of Hale'iwa. After the historic Hale'iwa Bridge, the entrance to the Hale'iwa Beach Park will be 0.3 mile away on the left.

From Kāne'ohe or Kailua, take H3 to the H1 west Pearl City

junction. Take H₁ west, and follow the directions above. From west O'ahu, take H1 east past Waikele. Take exit 8B east onto H2 north.

COURSE All three loops start and end at the Hale'iwa Beach Park. Begin the 4.1-mile loop by running along Kamehameha Highway back into Hale'iwa Town. After crossing the bridge, take the first right on Hale'iwa Road. Follow Hale'iwa Road past the Hale'iwa Boat Harbor and Hale'iwa Ali'i Beach Park. After 2 miles, Hale'iwa Road ends, and you will take a left on Waialua Beach Road. At the traffic circle, stay to the left, and follow Kamehameha Highway back into Hale'iwa. Run directly through the town of Hale'iwa, go over the bridge, and return to the beach park.

The 6.5-mile loop follows the same course as the shorter loop until Waialua Beach Road. At this point, turn right. After 0.3 mile turn left onto Goodale Avenue. Follow Goodale as it winds its way past the Waialua Elementary School and the Waialua Sugar Mill. At the bottom of the hill, turn left on Farrington Highway (930). After 0.7 mile and a short climb, turn left at Kaukonahua. Follow Kaukonahua back to the traffic circle. Again, stay left at the traffic circle, and take Kamehameha Highway back through Hale'iwa to the starting point at the beach park.

For the 10.7-mile loop, follow the 6.5-mile course, but continue straight along Waialua Beach Road past the Goodale Avenue cutoff. Waialua Beach Road eventually narrows to a single lane and finally ends at a gate. At this point, turn left on to Mahinaai. After a short 0.2 mile, Mahinaai ends at Farrington Highway, where you will turn left. Run along Farrington past the Waialua High and Intermediate Schools. Turn left onto Kaukonahua Road, eventually coming to the traffic circle. Again, stay to the left, and follow Kamehameha Highway back through Hale'iwa and to the beach park.

HIGHLIGHTS Hale'iwa has maintained much of its old charm from the early 1900s, when it began to develop into a small plantation town serving the Waialua sugar plantation workers. Prior to 1900, Benjamin Dillingham constructed the luxurious Hale'iwa Hotel in hopes of attracting more passengers for the railroad he had built to connect the north shore sugar mills with Honolulu. After World War II, the railroad closed, and Hale'iwa returned to a sleepy plantation town. In the early 1960s the surfing revolution exploded across the country, and Oʻahu's north shore quickly established it-self as the center of this revolution. As the only developed town on the north shore, Haleʻiwa benefited from its newfound popularity as a surfing mecca. Despite this instant popularity, Haleʻiwa suc-ceeded in maintaining much of its old plantation-town charm. A visit to Haleʻiwa is not complete without a visit to either Ma-tsumoto's or Aoki's stores for their famous Hawaiian shave ice. Noth-ing tops off a long run like a shave ice from Haleʻiwa.

CAUTIONS Haleʻiwa attracts many tourists, especially during the winter months, when the big north shore swells are breaking. Dur-ing these months, traffic can be heavy, so runners need to be aware that many of the drivers are more intent on sightseeing than in looking out for runners. As with many rural beach parks, cars are susceptible to break-ins, so be sure to lock your car, and leave your valuables at home. Streetlights are minimal in this rural town, so running after dark can be hazardous.

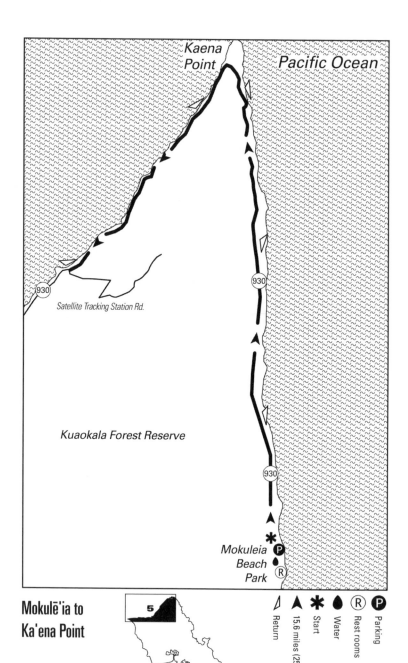

Kaena
Point

Pacific Ocean

930

Satellite Tracking Station Rd.

930

Kuaokala Forest Reserve

930

Mokuleia
Beach
Park

Mokulē'ia to
Ka'ena Point

5

Return

15.6 miles (25.1 km)

Start

Water

R Rest rooms

P Parking

MOKULĒ'IA TO KA'ENA POINT

DISTANCE:	*Medium to long out-and-back course, 5.6 to 15.6 miles (9.01 to 25.1 km)*
SURFACE:	*Blacktop; sand and rock trail*
SUITABLE FOR:	*Beginners on the paved road to the trailhead; intermediate to advanced runners for the trail section*
LOCATION:	*North Shore (Map Region 5)*
COURSE:	🀄 🀄 🀄 🀄
PARKING:	🀄 🀄 🀄
AMENITIES:	🀄 🀄
SAFETY:	🀄 🀄 🀄
OVERALL RATING:	🀄 🀄 🀄

OVERVIEW A beautiful stretch from Mokulē'ia to the Ka'ena Point trailhead along the rural northwestern coast, this route is well paved with a relatively wide shoulder. The paved road ends after 2.8 miles, and, for the next 5 miles, the route is a combination of sand and lava rock. Sections of the trail have been washed away by high surf, and some climbing is required. This isolated section of O'ahu is a great place to escape the crowds and get back to nature.

DIRECTIONS From Honolulu, leeward, and central O'ahu, take H1 to the H2 cutoff. Take H2 to Wahiawā. Take the Wahiawā exit north. Follow Highway 80 through Wahiawā, and merge with Highway 99 to the north shore. As you drop down from the plains of central O'ahu, take the Hale'iwa cutoff. Just beyond the cutoff is a traffic circle. Drive three-quarters around the circle, and take Kaukonahua Road (route 830) to Mokulē'ia. At the first stop sign, turn right on Farrington Highway (route 930) past Waialua High School. Continue straight on Farrington Highway. Mokulē'ia Beach Park is approximately 4.5 miles past the high school, across from the Dillingham Airfield.

COURSE From the Mokulēʻia Beach Park, follow Farrington Highway toward Kaʻena Point. The paved road will last for 2.8 miles and follows the coast along some beautiful and isolated beaches. The paved road is flat for the first 2.2 miles before it makes a few mild climbs to the beginning of the trail. Turn around at the end of the road, and return to the beach park for a 5.6-mile run.

For a longer and much more challenging run, continue past the gate at the trailhead, and head out along the trail around Kaʻena Point. This trail should not be attempted after dark, as footing can be quite hazardous. Follow the trail around the point and back toward Mākua on the Waiʻanae Coast. At the end of the trail, turn around, and head back to the start point. The trail section is 5 miles one-way, so the entire out-and-back course to Mokulēʻia is 15.6 miles.

HIGHLIGHTS This route is a great escape from the congestion that impacts much of Oʻahu. Except for some shoreline fishermen and folks heading out to do a little four-wheeling, very few vehicles drive out this way. This route offers beautiful shoreline views throughout. It might be well worth the trouble to bring along a small camera. Kaʻena Point was designated a Natural Area Reserve in 1983, protected for its wide range of native plants, insects, and birds, so be sure to stay on the marked paths. The endangered plants and wildlife are slowly making a comeback in this area. Kaʻena Point is also one of the best places on Oʻahu to spot the endangered monk seal. Historically, Kaʻena Point has held an important role in Hawaiiana as a "liena," or a jumping-off point where the spirits of the dead would leap into the next world. Dillingham Airfield is the site for glider rides and parachuting, so if you are up for some airborne adventure after your run, head across the street from Mokulēʻia, and check with the folks at the airfield.

CAUTIONS The isolated appeal of this course also means that cars left at the beach park are susceptible to break-ins. Do not leave valuables in your car. The trail portion of this run can be hazardous in areas where the trail has been washed away by high surf. Due to these washouts, do not attempt this trail after dark. Ropes have been placed in areas that have suffered from washouts to help runners climb around these sections. Be aware that during the winter months, high surf is common along this stretch. Check the daily surf reports before heading out around the point. No shade trees or water sources are along the 5-mile trail, so be sure to use sunscreen, and bring your own water supply.

This route is especially pretty at sunrise and sunset; however, if you choose to run this course during sunset, be aware that this section of Oʻahu has no streetlights and gets extremely dark, so plan accordingly.

The road around Kaʻena Point is listed as off-limits for vehicular traffic, but that does not discourage the adventurous folks in their four-wheel-drive trucks and dirt bikes, who still use portions of the trail. Don't be surprised to run into some monster trucks along the early stages of the trail. Also, keep an eye out for ATVs, because they don't expect to see runners along this route.

REGION 6

LEEWARD SIDE

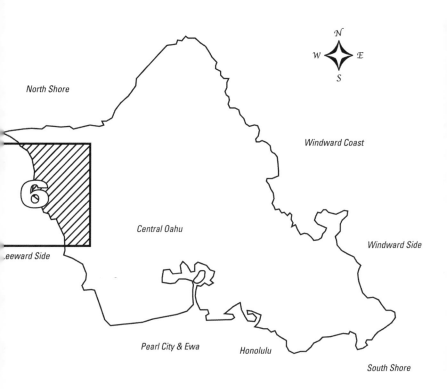

North Shore

Windward Coast

Central Oahu

Windward Side

Leeward Side

Pearl City & Ewa

Honolulu

South Shore

N
W   E
S

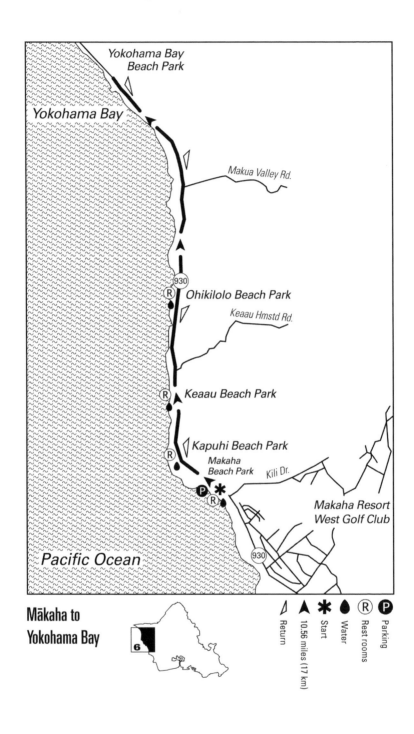

Yokohama Bay
Beach Park

Yokohama Bay

Makua Valley Rd.

930

Ⓡ Ohikilolo Beach Park

Keaau Hmstd Rd.

Ⓡ Keaau Beach Park

Ⓡ Kapuhi Beach Park

*Makaha
Beach Park* *Kili Dr.*

Ⓟ
Ⓡ

Makaha Resort
West Golf Club

930

Pacific Ocean

Mākaha to
Yokohama Bay

6

Return

10.56 miles (17 km)

Start

Water

Ⓡ Rest rooms

Ⓟ Parking

MĀKAHA TO YOKOHAMA BAY

DISTANCE:	*Short to medium course, up to 10.56 miles (17 km) (All distances listed below are out-and-back.)*
	MĀKAHA
	—to Kapuhi Beach Park = 2 miles (3.2 km)
	—to Keaʻau Beach Park = 2.8 miles (4.5 km)
	—to ʻŌhikilolo Beach Park = 4 miles (6.44 km)
	—to Mākua = 7.4 miles (11.9 km)
	—to Yokohama Bay = 10.56 miles (17 km)
SURFACE:	*Blacktop and cement sidewalks; flat*
SUITABLE FOR:	*All levels*
LOCATION:	*Leeward Side (Map Region 6)*
COURSE:	🩴 🩴 🩴
PARKING:	🩴 🩴 🩴
AMENITIES:	🩴 🩴
SAFETY:	🩴 🩴
OVERALL RATING:	🩴 🩴 🩴

OVERVIEW This out-and-back shoreline course runs along the uppermost portion of the leeward coast. Relatively flat with some minor hills, this route can be run entirely on sidewalks and paved roadway. A number of beach parks are spread out along this route, and each offers public rest rooms and water. Parking is available at Mākaha Beach Park, but, as with all parking in this area, you should not leave valuables in your car. The leeward coast is attractive, bordered on one side by a combination of long stretches of white sand beach and rocky coastline and on the other by the Waiʻanae Mountains and deep, dry valleys. You can choose to turn around at Yokohama Bay (also known as Keawaʻula Bay), or continue to the point where the paved road ends.

DIRECTIONS From all parts of the island, take H1 west to Wai‘a-nae on the leeward coast. Just after the Ko Olina exit, H1 ends and becomes Farrington Highway (930). Follow Farrington Highway through Nānākuli, Wai‘anae, and Mākaha, and park at Mākaha Beach Park.

COURSE This route is quite simple. Start at Mākaha Beach Park, and run north along Farrington Highway (930) toward the upper-most tip of O‘ahu. Run facing traffic at all times. This course will take you along the leeward coast past a number of beach parks. You can choose to run all the way to the point where Farrington High-way ends, which is 5.28 miles, and return for a 10.56-mile run, or you can choose a shorter distance by using any of the beach parks as a turnaround point.

HIGHLIGHTS The primary highlight of this route is the stunning coastline of white sand beaches intermingled with outcroppings of black rock. The leeward coast is bordered by the 20-mile-long Wai‘anae Mountain Range, which includes the 4,030-foot Mount Ka‘ala, the highest point on O‘ahu. These mountains block most of the rain brought in by the trade winds, resulting in dry and sunny valleys along this stretch. When the agriculture industry flourished on O‘ahu, a railway line connected the leeward coast with the rest of O‘ahu's North Shore. After the railroad was abandoned, leeward O‘ahu became a dead end, and, until recently, efforts to develop resorts in this area had failed. However, the Ko Olina Resorts opened in the 1990s and have seen some success. Recently Ko Olina has started to expand, constructing extensive luxury time-share and town house complexes surrounded by a spectacular championship golf course and four man-made lagoons.

CAUTIONS The leeward coast is dry and hot, and, even though the running route is on the water, the trade winds are coming from off-shore and are mostly blocked by the Wai‘anae Mountains. This route is best during the early morning hours or just prior to sun-down. Again, break-ins are a problem in this area, so do not park in a secluded place, and do not leave valuables in your car.

CENTRAL O'AHU

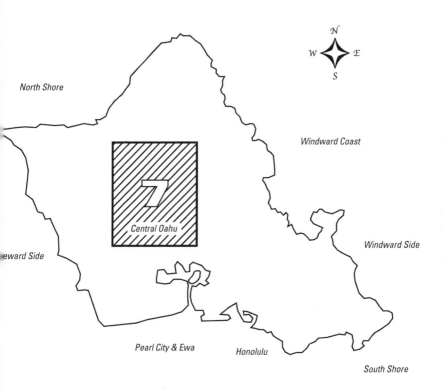

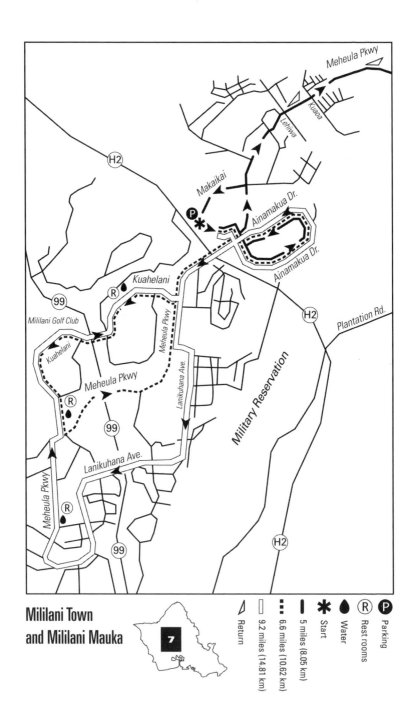

**Mililani Town
and Mililani Mauka**

7

Return
9.2 miles (14.81 km)
6.6 miles (10.62 km)
5 miles (8.05 km)
✳ Start
◗ Water
Ⓡ Rest rooms
Ⓟ Parking

Meheula Pkwy

Kuaoa

Lehiwa

Makaikai

Ⓟ
✳

Ainamakua Dr.

Ainamakua Dr.

H2

Kuahelani

Ⓡ

99

Mililani Golf Club

Kuahelani

Meheula Pkwy

Lanikuhana Ave.

Meheula Pkwy

Ⓡ

99

H2

Plantation Rd.

Military Reservation

Lanikuhana Ave.

Meheula Pkwy

Ⓡ

99

H2

MILILANI TOWN AND MILILANI MAUKA

DISTANCE:	*5, 6.6, or 9.2 miles (8.05, 10.62, or 14.81 km)*
SURFACE:	*Sidewalks; hilly*
SUITABLE FOR:	*All levels*
LOCATION:	*Central Oʻahu (Map Region 7)*
COURSE:	🏃 🏃 🏃 🏃
PARKING:	🏃 🏃 🏃 🏃
AMENITIES:	🏃 🏃 🏃
SAFETY:	🏃 🏃 🏃 🏃
OVERALL RATING:	🏃 🏃 🏃 🏃

OVERVIEW Mililani Town is a mature, tree-lined, planned community developed in 1968 by Castle and Cooke. Mililani Mauka is the more recent development, separated from the original Mililani Town by the H2 interstate. Mililani is situated in the highlands of central Oʻahu, providing slightly cooler temperatures and a break from the daytime heat of Honolulu. This planned community offers 6 recreation centers, along with 21 parks and plenty of designated walking and running paths. The roads are all well lit and lined with sidewalks providing safe day or nighttime running. The three courses described are just a sample of the various routes available in the Mililani area, each of which offers convenient parking and crosses a limited number of major intersections. All of the courses in Mililani include some hills.

DIRECTIONS From Honolulu, take H1 west past Pearl City. After passing the Waipahu exit, stay in the right lane, and take the H2 north cutoff. From H2, take the Mililani Mauka exit. From the exit, you will merge with the Meheʻula Parkway. Move to the far-left lane, and turn left at the first traffic light on ʻĀinamakua Drive. From ʻĀinamakua, take the first left on Ukuwai, and park in the

Park-and-Ride parking area. From the north shore, take H2 south to Mililani exit 5. Turn left on Mehe'ula Parkway, cross over H2, and follow the directions listed above.

COURSE All three courses start at the same location, the Park-and-Ride parking area just off the H2 exit on the edge of Mililani Mauka. Rest rooms and drinks are available at the McDonalds, and a mini-mart is located adjacent to the parking area.

The first course is 5 miles, stays entirely in the Mililani Mauka subdivision, and includes a long, mild climb and descent. From the Park-and-Ride, turn right on Ukuwai Road, and take another right on 'Āinamakua. Cross the Mehe'ula Parkway, and continue on 'Āinamakua as it makes a long loop to the left. As you complete the loop, turn right back on 'Āinamakua after 1.5 miles. After 0.2 mile, turn right on the Mehe'ula Parkway, and follow the parkway up a long grade for 1.4 miles until you reach upper Lehiwa Drive. At this point, turn around, and head back the way you came. At the fire station on Māka'ika'i Road, turn right, and follow Māka'ika'i back to the Park-and-Ride.

The 6.6-mile run starts at the same Park-and-Ride, but when you reach the Mehe'ula Parkway, turn right, and follow the parkway across the H2 overpass toward Mililani Town. After 1.1 miles, turn right on Kuahelani Avenue. At the 1.4-mile mark is the Kīpapa Park, with rest rooms and water. Continue along Kuahelani, and cross Kamehameha Highway (99). At the 2.3-mile mark, you will pass the Mililani Golf Course entrance. After the golf course, turn left on Mehe'ula Parkway, cross Kamehameha Highway again, and continue past the Mililani High School and Town Center shopping area back toward Mililani Mauka. After the H2 overpass, turn right on 'Āinamakua Drive, and follow the 'Āinamakua loop back to the Mehe'ula Parkway. Cross the parkway, and return to the Park-and-Ride.

The final course is a 9.2-mile run that includes some long hills and starts in the same direction as the second course. Continue on Mehe'ula Parkway past Kuahelani. Turn left on Ho'okelewa'a Street. After one block, this street name changes to Lanikūhana Avenue. Follow Lanikūhana down a long hill, and cross Kamehameha Highway. Shortly after crossing Kamehameha Highway, you will pass Mililani District Park on your right. Rest rooms and water are accessible at the park. At approximately 4 miles, turn right on Mehe'ula Parkway. Follow the parkway up a slight incline for 1 mile, and turn left on Kuahelani Avenue. Continue past the golf course, and cross Kamehameha Highway. A half-mile past Kamehameha Highway is Kīpapa Park, with rest rooms and water. Turn left on Mehe'ula Parkway, and return across the H2 overpass. As with the second course, after crossing H2, turn right at 'Āinamakua, and finish off the run with the 'Āinamakua loop before crossing Mehe'ula and returning to the Park-and-Ride.

HIGHLIGHTS Mililani Town and Mililani Mauka are well-designed developments that are beautifully landscaped and include many shade trees along its winding roads. The combination of shade trees and higher elevation make Mililani an excellent place to run during the hot summer months. Mililani is also a clean and well-maintained community, and neighborhood traffic tends to be light. The heaviest traffic is usually on Kamehameha Highway, so caution is advised when crossing this busy thoroughfare.

CAUTIONS All three courses are designed to provide the least number of major intersection crossings, but you cannot avoid a few major intersections. Be careful crossing Kamehameha Highway and Mehe'ula Parkway. Mililani has very few straight roads and can be quite confusing to the uninitiated. If you are new to the Mililani area, you may want to drive each of the courses first to become familiar with the courses and the challenging road names.

PEARL CITY AND 'EWA

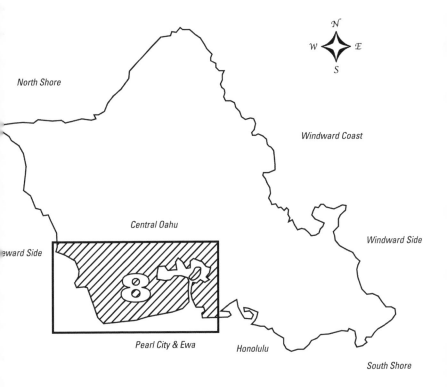

North Shore

Central Oahu

eward Side

Pearl City & Ewa

Honolulu

Windward Coast

Windward Side

South Shore

N

W *E*

S

8

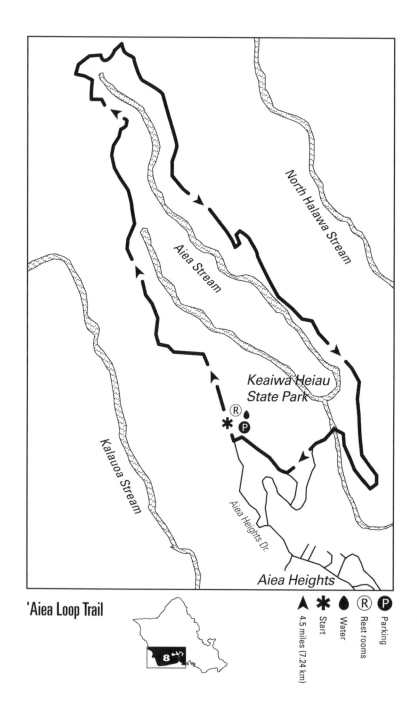

'Aiea Loop Trail

North Halawa Stream

Aiea Stream

Kalauoa Stream

Keaiwa Heiau
State Park

Aiea Heights Dr.

Aiea Heights

8

▲ 4.5 miles (7.24 km)
✳ Start
💧 Water
Ⓡ Rest rooms
🅿 Parking

'AIEA LOOP TRAIL

DISTANCE:	*4.5 miles (7.24 km)*
SURFACE:	*Dirt trail; exposed roots; hilly*
SUITABLE FOR:	*All levels*
LOCATION:	*Pearl City and 'Ewa (Map Region 8)*
PARK HOURS:	*Park gate hours are 7:00 AM–6:45 PM.*
COURSE:	🥾🥾🥾🥾
PARKING:	🥾🥾🥾🥾
AMENITIES:	🥾🥾🥾
SAFETY:	🥾🥾🥾
OVERALL RATING:	🥾🥾🥾

OVERVIEW A short, fun, 4.5-mile loop trail, this course is situated at the top of 'Aiea Heights Drive in the Keaīwa Heiau State Recreation Area. This trail is extremely popular with hikers and mountain bikers, so take care when approaching blind turns. Due to the 1,000-foot elevation of this trail, the temperatures are always cool, making it a perfect summer run. A number of parking areas are spread throughout the park, and a picnic area, a rest room, and a water fountain are at the trailhead. This trail gets muddy, so leave your new shoes home. Trail shoes are highly recommended.

DIRECTIONS From Honolulu, take H1 west to the Hālawa and Stadium exit. At the second traffic light, continue straight across Hālawa Heights Road onto Ulune Street. Follow Ulune Street until it ends at 'Aiea Heights Drive. Turn right, and follow 'Aiea Heights Drive as it winds its way to the top of the ridge. Enter the Keaīwa Heiau State Recreation Area, and continue past the *heiau* and the camping area to the uppermost parking area.

From windward O'ahu, take H3 to the Hālawa and Stadium exit. Continue straight at the traffic light on Ulune Street. At the end of Ulune Street, turn right on 'Aiea Heights Drive, and continue to the Keaīwa Heiau entrance. Drive through the entrance, and stay on the road to the very top of the hill.

COURSE From the trailhead, there is a short, steep descent over exposed roots, then the trail begins a slight but steady climb for the next 1.5 miles. Along this stretch a number of lookout points give a great excuse for you to take a breather and allow your heart rate to recover. Also, two large trees have fallen across the trail at different points, so duck low enough to clear these trees. There is nothing like a big lump on your head to ruin a perfectly good trail run. Shortly after you clear the second tree, the trail turns to the right and starts downhill. The drop is gentle and provides for a smooth recovery from the earlier climb. The trail has now switched over to the opposite side of the ridge and offers some excellent viewpoints of the Hālawa Valley and the ribbon of H3 connecting Pearl Harbor with Kāneʻohe Bay. The trail continues to descend to the valley floor. After crossing a small stream, the trail starts a steady climb with a number of switchbacks until it opens up to a small grass clearing that serves as a campsite. Take the steps on the right that lead back to the road. Turn right, and follow the road for a 0.25-mile climb back to the starting point at the upper trailhead.

HIGHLIGHTS This trail is well maintained and safe for all levels of runners. A few trails split off from the main trail and add variety. The first trail, Kalauao Trail, takes off to the left shortly after you pass a powerline tower. Due to the muddy conditions and steep descents, this trail is not good for running, but a beautiful waterfall and pool at the base make this short but challenging out-and-back trip a worthwhile diversion. The second trail splits off to the left at the 1.6-mile mark. This is the ʻAiea Ridge Trail, an 11-mile out-and-back trip that follows the ridge to the Koʻolau Ridge Summit and a magnificent view of windward Oʻahu. As with the Kalauao Trail, the ʻAiea Ridge Trail is not recommended as a running trail due to its long, narrow stretches that may be treacherous. Back on the main loop trail around the 2.5-mile mark, you can spot pieces of a C-47 Army transport, all that is left from a fiery crash that occurred back in 1943. After your run, stop by the remains of the Keaīwa Heiau at the entrance to the park. This *heiau* was an ancient temple believed to have been used by Hawaiian healers.

CAUTIONS Many hikers and bicyclists also use this trail. Be careful to keep an eye out for them, and let them know you are coming. You will also find stretches that have exposed roots, which can be quite slippery. The trail can get muddy at times, and exposed rocks may be slick, but that's what makes trail-running so much fun. If you wanted dry, flat surfaces, you would stick to running along Ala Moana Boulevard.

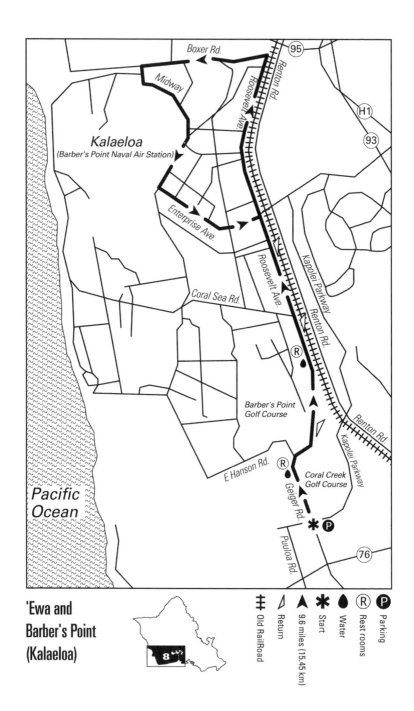

'Ewa and Barber's Point (Kalaeloa)

Boxer Rd.
Midway
Roosevelt Ave.
Renton Rd.
95
H1
93
Kalaeloa
(Barber's Point Naval Air Station)
Enterprise Ave.
Roosevelt Ave.
Kapolei Parkway
Renton Rd.
Coral Sea Rd.
R
Barber's Point
Golf Course
Renton Rd.
E Hanson Rd.
R
Coral Creek
Golf Course
Kapolei Parkway
Pacific
Ocean
Geiger Rd.
76
Puuloa Rd.
P

8

‡ Old RailRoad
／ Return
▲ 9.6 miles (15.45 km)
✳ Start
⬤ Water
Ⓡ Rest rooms
Ⓟ Parking

'EWA AND BARBER'S POINT (KALAELOA)

DISTANCE:	*9.6 miles (15.45 km)*
SURFACE:	*Blacktop; wide crushed coral shoulders*
SUITABLE FOR:	*Intermediate to advanced*
LOCATION:	*Pearl City and 'Ewa (Map Region 8)*
COURSE:	🚶 🚶 🚶 🚶
PARKING:	🚶 🚶 🚶 🚶
AMENITIES:	🚶 🚶 🚶
SAFETY:	🚶 🚶 🚶 🚶
OVERALL RATING:	🚶 🚶 🚶 🚶

OVERVIEW This flat, long course takes you through the old Barber's Point Naval Air Station, now known as the Kalaeloa Community Development District. You won't find any traffic or major intersections, and plenty of public rest rooms and water stations are available along the route.

DIRECTIONS From H1, take the 'Ewa exit. Follow Fort Weaver Road toward 'Ewa Beach. Turn right on Geiger Road. At the corner of Geiger Road and Kapolei Parkway is Geiger Park, which is the starting point. Geiger Park does not have a parking lot, but street parking is available in the surrounding neighborhood.

COURSE From the corner of Geiger Road and Kapolei Parkway, head out along Geiger Road toward the former Barber's Point Naval Air Station. Geiger Road has wide shoulders of crushed coral. Pass the entrance of Coral Creek Golf Course, where water is available at the clubhouse. Just past the golf course is the old back gate of the naval air station. At the gate, Geiger Road becomes Roosevelt Avenue. Continue straight on Roosevelt. At approximately 1.7 miles you will pass a Little League baseball field with rest rooms and water on your left.

At 2.8 miles, you will reach the old main gate. Continue straight on Roosevelt past the main gate. At approximately 4 miles, just before the end of Roosevelt, turn left on Boxer Road. After about 1 mile, Boxer Road will take you past the Navy Fitness Center and batting cages. The fitness center offers public rest rooms and water. Shortly after the fitness center, you will pass the Hawai'i Air Museum in Hangar 111. Boxer Road will then pass the Air Traffic Control Tower and veer to the left. After the left bend, Boxer becomes Midway Road. At 6 miles, Midway turns left at a chain-link fence and continues to Enterprise Road. Turn left on Enterprise. Enterprise passes another baseball complex that offers public rest rooms and water, and it will take you back to the main gate. Here, turn right on Roosevelt, and head back the way you came, returning through the back gate to Geiger Road, then continue on to Geiger Park.

HIGHLIGHTS This course is a great place to train without having to deal with traffic. Decommissioned in 1999, this old, 3,600-acre naval base still houses some military personnel but, for the most part, has been handed over to the state of Hawai'i, which hopes to use this acreage as an economic development zone. Miles of paved roads and no traffic are perfect for escaping the crowds and putting in some long, uninterrupted training runs.

CAUTIONS The 'Ewa plains are hot and dry. This route offers a number of water stations along the way, but you still might want to bring your own source of fluids. Due to the heat, this route is best suited for the early morning or early evening. There are no streetlights through the old Barber's Point Naval Station, so it is not recommended for nighttime runs. The coral shoulder provides a cooler and softer running surface, but crushed coral will wear out the soles of your running shoes faster than most surfaces. Finally, now that the state of Hawai'i has taken over this land, discussions are under way to rename all the streets with Hawaiian names. At the time of this printing, the street names listed in the directions above are still active.

'EWA AND WEST LOCH BIKE PATH

DISTANCE:	*4 miles (6.44 km)*
SURFACE:	*Bike path*
SUITABLE FOR:	*All levels*
LOCATION:	*Pearl City and 'Ewa (Map Region 8)*
PARK HOURS:	*Open from 7:00 AM to 7:00 PM*
COURSE:	🏃 🏃 🏃 🏃 🏃
PARKING:	🏃 🏃 🏃 🏃
AMENITIES:	🏃 🏃 🏃 🏃
SAFETY:	🏃 🏃 🏃 🏃 🏃
OVERALL RATING:	🏃 🏃 🏃 🏃 🏃

OVERVIEW This gem is hidden away behind the West Loch Estates in 'Ewa. At some point this bike path will be extended to connect with the Pearl Harbor Bike Path, but until that happens this wide, little-used path is a great place to escape the crowds and enjoy a short, peaceful run. Rest rooms and water are available at the West Loch Shoreline Park and the Asing Community Park.

DIRECTIONS From H1 west, take the 'Ewa exit. Follow Fort Weaver Road in the direction of 'Ewa Beach. Turn left into West Loch Estates (Laulaunui Road). Drive past the entrance for West Loch Golf Course, and turn at the second right into the West Loch Shoreline Park.

COURSE From the West Loch Shoreline Park parking area, turn left on the bike path for a 1.5-mile loop. Head up a short hill, and be sure to stay to the right each time the path splits. Follow the shoreline until the path ends at the park's caretaker's home. At this point, run up a short but steep hill. This short access road comes out onto Kaihuopala'ai Street. Turn right, and then take a quick left on 'Ama'ama. Another quick left on Kapapapuhi Street will take you

143

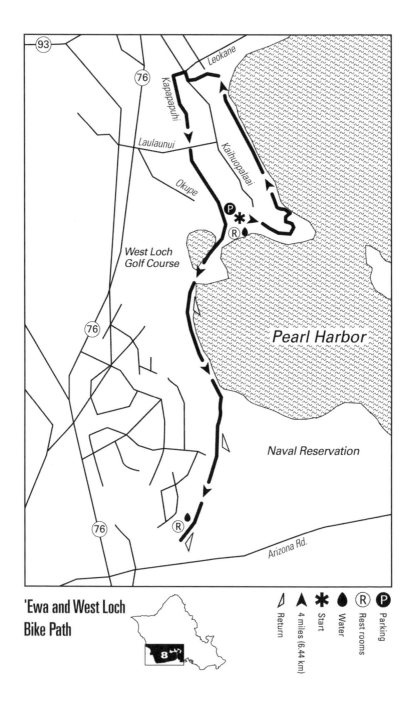

93

76

Leokane

Kapapapuhi

Laulaunui

Okupe

Kaihuopalaai

P

✳

R

West Loch
Golf Course

Pearl Harbor

76

Naval Reservation

76

R

Arizona Rd.

'Ewa and West Loch
Bike Path

8

Return   4 miles (6.44 km)   Start   Water   R Rest rooms   P Parking

down an attractive, tree-lined road that leads straight back to the West Loch Shoreline Park. Return to where the first loop started, but this time turn right, and follow the bike path in the opposite direction. This portion of the bike path runs for 1.25 miles and borders the West Loch Golf Course. The paved path ends in the West Loch Fairways neighborhood at the Asing Community Park, which offers a new public recreation center with rest rooms and water. At this point, turn around, and head back in the direction you came to complete a 4-mile run.

HIGHLIGHTS This waterfront run has no traffic, no intersections, and very few people. Since it is relatively unknown, this course is a great way to escape from the crowds. If these short bike paths aren't long enough for you, continue on a short dirt path to the left of the Asing Community Park. Here you will find a deserted sugarcane field with miles and miles of paved roads. You can combine a variety of these roads to make an extremely long, flat run. If you choose to run the cane field roads, be sure to bring your own supply of fluids because these fields tend to get hot during the day.

CAUTIONS No lights are along the bike path, so this is strictly a daytime run. The best time to schedule a run is early morning or early evening because the 'Ewa plains get quite hot. Offshore breezes help defuse some of the heat, but, when the path leaves the coast, there is little heat relief.

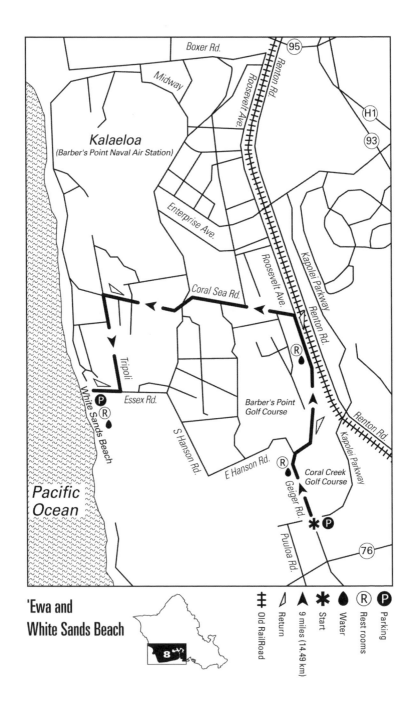

Boxer Rd.

95

Midway

Renton Rd.

Roosevelt Ave.

H1

93

Kalaeloa
(Barber's Point Naval Air Station)

Enterprise Ave.

Coral Sea Rd.

Roosevelt Ave.

Kapolei Parkway

Renton Rd.

Ⓡ

Tripoli

White Sands Beach

Ⓟ
Ⓡ

Essex Rd.

Barber's Point
Golf Course

S Hanson Rd.

Renton Rd.

Pacific
Ocean

E Hanson Rd.

Ⓡ

Geiger Rd.

Coral Creek
Golf Course

Kapolei Parkway

✱ Ⓟ

Puuloa Rd.

76

'Ewa and
White Sands Beach

8

‡ Old RailRoad
⁄ Return
▲ 9 miles (14.49 km)
✱ Start
⬤ Water
Ⓡ Rest rooms
Ⓟ Parking

'EWA AND WHITE SANDS BEACH

DISTANCE:	*Medium out-and-back course, up to 9 miles (14.49 km)*
SURFACE:	*Blacktop; wide crushed coral shoulders*
SUITABLE FOR:	*Intermediate to advanced*
LOCATION:	*Pearl City and 'Ewa (Map Region 8)*
COURSE:	👟 👟 👟 👟
PARKING:	👟 👟 👟 👟
AMENITIES:	👟 👟 👟
SAFETY:	👟 👟 👟 👟
OVERALL RATING:	👟 👟 👟 👟

OVERVIEW This out-and-back course runs from Geiger Park to White Sands Beach in the old Barber's Point Naval Air Station, now known as the Kalaeloa Community Development District. This completely flat route can be paved blacktop or on shoulders made of crushed white coral. There is little traffic throughout the entire park. Rest rooms and water are available at Geiger Park and White Sands Beach Park, as well as the Coral Creek Golf clubhouse and the baseball field along the course.

DIRECTIONS As with the 'Ewa and Barber's Point run, from H1, take the 'Ewa exit. Follow Fort Weaver Road toward 'Ewa Beach. Turn right on Geiger Road. At the corner of Geiger Road and Kapolei Parkway is Geiger Park, which is the starting point. Geiger Park does not have a parking lot, but street parking is available in the surrounding neighborhood.

COURSE From Geiger Park, take Geiger Road toward Kalaeloa (formerly known as Barber's Point Naval Air Station). When entering Kalaeloa, Geiger Road becomes Roosevelt Avenue. Continue on Roosevelt Avenue. After passing a baseball field on your left, take the first left on Coral Sea Road. Continue along Coral Sea Road until Tripoli Road. Turn left on Tripoli, and then turn right on White Sands Beach Road, which ends at the beach park parking area. White Sands Beach offers safe swimming, rest rooms, water, showers, and a snack bar. From the beach park, turn around, and return on the same route for a flat 9 miles.

HIGHLIGHTS Named after a British sea captain who wrecked his ship off this point in 1796, Barber's Point Naval Air Station was commissioned in 1942 and soon grew into the largest naval air station in the Pacific, with more than 6,500 personnel. Focused primarily on anti-submarine warfare, the air station's importance declined with the end of the Cold War. In the mid-1990s, rampant military base consolidations and closures took place. Barber's Point was the final victim of the twentieth century and was decommissioned in 1999. The Hawai'i State Legislature took over 2,150 acres of the base, earmarking 500 acres for use as Hawaiian Home Lands, and the remaining acreage and airfield became the Kalaeloa Community Development District. Renamed Kalaeloa after the original Hawaiian name for this point (long cape or headland) and open to the public, this area offers 2 miles of white sand beaches and numerous sparsely traveled roads that are great for running and biking. White Sands Beach serves as a great turnaround point, with public rest rooms and a snack bar that is open on weekends.

CAUTIONS As with the 'Ewa and Barber's Point route, the 'Ewa plains are hot and dry, so bring your own fluids. The snack bar at the White Sands Beach Park is open only on weekends, so don't count on it during your weekday runs. The Kalaeloa area lacks streetlights, so this course is not recommended after dark.

PEARL CITY BIKE PATH

DISTANCE:	*Medium out-and-back course, 5.85 or 11.7 miles (9.41 or 18.83 km)*
SURFACE:	*Blacktop; flat*
SUITABLE FOR:	*All levels*
LOCATION:	*Pearl City and ʻEwa (Map Region 8)*
COURSE:	中 中 中
PARKING:	中 中 中
AMENITIES:	中 中 中
SAFETY:	中 中 中 中
OVERALL RATING:	中 中 中

OVERVIEW The Pearl City and ʻAiea areas are some of the most densely populated areas on Oʻahu. Along with all those people come many confusing and congested roadways, the combination of which places severe limits on the options for safe and continuous running courses. The Pearl City Bike Path, which starts just to the right of the USS *Bowfin* Submarine Museum at the Arizona Memorial Visitor's Center, is the best option. This flat, two-lane bike course borders the shoreline of Pearl Harbor and extends to Waipahu. This path is heavily traveled, so stay to the far right, and be observant of bikers and strollers.

DIRECTIONS From Honolulu, take the H1 airport viaduct. Pass Honolulu International Airport, and follow signs for the Arizona Memorial. Exit on Kamehameha Highway (99). Follow Kamehameha Highway, and turn left into the Arizona Memorial entrance. Turn right at the bottom of a short hill, and proceed to the parking area next to the boat docks. From windward Oʻahu, take H3, exiting at the Hālawa and Stadium exit. Continue straight at the traffic light onto Ulune Street. Follow Ulune until it ends, and turn left, then cross over H1, and turn left on Moanalua Road. At the first traffic light, two lanes turn right. Turn right, but stay in the left lane. Continue straight over the next overpass, passing

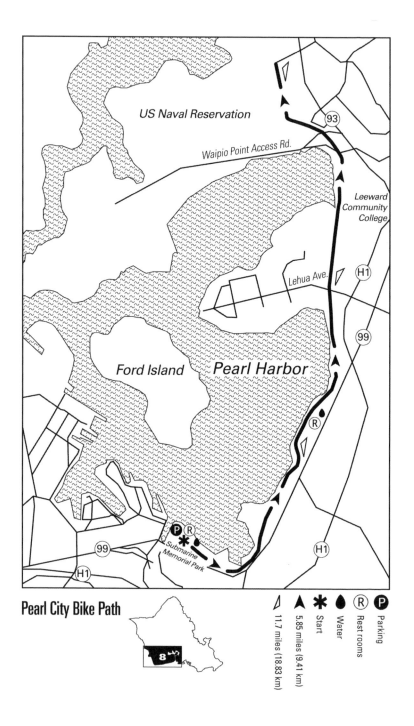

US Naval Reservation

Waipio Point Access Rd.

Leeward Community College

Lehua Ave.

Ford Island

Pearl Harbor

Submarine Memorial Park

Pearl City Bike Path

11.7 miles (18.83 km)

5.85 miles (9.41 km)

Start

Water

Rest rooms

Parking

Aloha Stadium on your left. This road will merge with Kamehameha Highway. Continue straight on Kamehameha, and follow the signs for the Arizona Memorial Visitor's Center.

COURSE A flat, two-lane bike path that runs along the fringe of Pearl Harbor. Start at the boat harbor next to the Arizona Memorial Visitor's Center, and follow the path as it winds its way between the harbor and the industrial park of 'Aiea and lower Pearl City. The path ends at Waipahu Depot Road. The bike path will take you through the 'Aiea Bay State Recreation Area, the Neal Blaisdell Park, and the Pearl City Kai Playground. Each of these parks provides rest rooms and water stations.

HIGHLIGHTS Despite its historic location, this route is not especially attractive. It does, however, offer a safe place to run while avoiding the heavily traveled roads in this densely populated area. Another nice feature is that the bike path has many friendly regulars who make newcomers feel welcome. The Arizona Memorial and the USS *Bowfin* Submarine Museum are a must-see when you are in the area. The Arizona Memorial Visitor's Center is also where you can sign up for a tour of the USS *Missouri*. Across Kamehameha Highway from the Arizona Memorial is Aloha Stadium, the home of the University of Hawai'i Football team, as well as the site for the annual NFL Pro Bowl. The Mid-Pacific Road Runners Club hosts a 10K race on the bike path each spring, and the bike path is also used as part of the O'ahu Perimeter Relay, held in February of each year.

CAUTION Since this is a bike path, you don't need to worry about automobile traffic, but pedestrian traffic can get heavy. Be considerate, and stay as far to the right as possible to prevent any run-ins with bicycles.

ABOUT THE AUTHOR

Richard Varley received his MA in history from East Stroudsburg University in Pennsylvania in 1982. He is currently the director of Internship and Career Development in the College of Business Administration at University of Hawaiʻi at Mānoa. An avid runner and triathlete, he competed in fifteen marathons, as well as numerous road races, relays, and triathlons. He is the founder and president of the Mānoa Road Runners, a registered independent organization at the University of Hawaiʻi. Since 2001, he has served as a running coach and program coordinator for Team Jet Hawaiʻi Running and Triathlon Club.